dBASE III Plus

D. SOBEY

dBASE III Plus
Training Guide

Jeanne MacInnes

Pitman Publishing

PITMAN PUBLISHING
128 Long Acre, London, WC2E 9AN

Pitman Publishing
A Division of Longman Group UK Limited

First published in Great Britain 1989
Reprinted 1990, 1991 (twice), 1992

British Library Cataloguing in Publication Data
DBase III plus
1. Microcomputer systems. Machine – readable files. Management. Software packages: DBase III plus
005.75'65

ISBN 0 273 03054 X

Printed and bound in Great Britain

Contents

Introduction

The purpose of this training guide is to introduce the user to the basics of dBASE III Plus with the minimum of instruction.

A series of tasks allows the user to learn the basic facilities and put them into practice by carrying out the activities that follow.

A database is a collection of records, all containing the same sort of information and arranged in such a way that obtaining information from them is made easy. Examples of printed databases that you might have used are telephone directories, address books, holiday brochures, price lists, etc. A computer database that you may have seen is the on-line booking system at a travel agency.

Let us take a price list as an example: reading down a price list, each line can be regarded as a RECORD. Looking along each line you will probably see an Item Code, Description, Size, and Price. These four items are the record's FIELDS and they appear on each and every line. Furthermore, the price list will have been printed in some logical order for ease of reference, perhaps in item code sequence, divided into sections according to product type. In this example, the item code is the KEY FIELD; i.e. it uniquely identifies each record and is normally used to sequence the file.

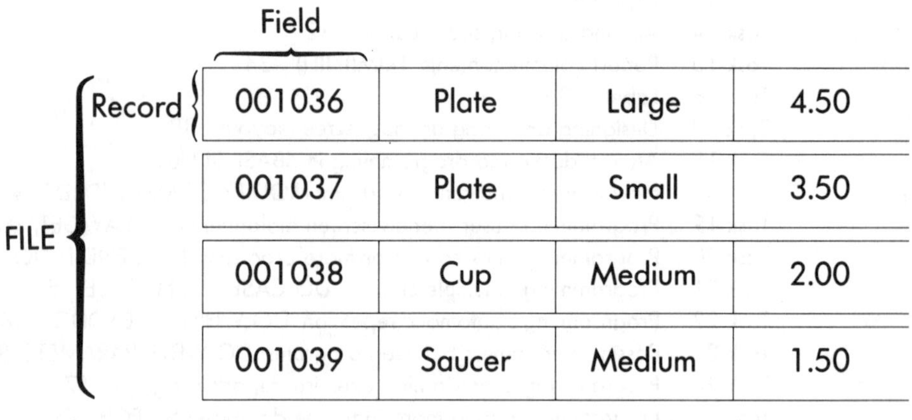

Field

FILE

	Field			
Record	001036	Plate	Large	4.50
	001037	Plate	Small	3.50
	001038	Cup	Medium	2.00
	001039	Saucer	Medium	1.50

dBASE III Plus enables you to create, arrange, alter, and use your own databases on disk by means of simple COMMANDS. It also allows you to design your own screen and report layouts with some ease.

Once you have gained experience in the use of these commands, you can go on to build complex PROGRAMS from them.

In this guide

dBASE III Plus allows you to give your commands in two ways: either by typing them in at the 'dot' (.) prompt on screen, or by selecting them from the assist menu.

It is easier to learn what the commands are and what they do by entering them yourself using the dot prompt, than by moving the cursor about the assist menu and pressing the RETURN key as instructed. This guide will, therefore, give instructions for the dot prompt commands only.

Commands are shown in the dBase III Plus Manual in the following format:

COMMAND [<scope>] [<expression list>] [FOR <condition>]

– [square] brackets indicate that the parameters within are optional;
Note Parameters are the additional information, following, and required by, each command to enable the user to carry out the function.
– <pointed> brackets indicate that the parameters within are to be specified by you;
– COMMANDs are shown in capital letters, but you can choose upper or lower case.
This format will be used in the exercises in this training guide.
Once you have mastered the basics in this training guide, you will find the assist menu easy to understand, and from then on you will have the choice of either method.

dBase always reminds you that you are at the dot prompt by displaying 'Enter a dBASE III Plus Command' at the foot of the screen.

For readability, the term 'dBase' will be used frequently in the instructions as a shortened version of 'dBase III Plus'

Sometimes you need to use the CTRL key in conjunction with another key. This will be shown as CTRL– (for example, CTRL–END means 'press the CTRL and END keys together').
RETURN is used to indicate 'Press the , or ENTER key'.

If you make a typing error at the dot prompt, dBASE will ask: 'Do you want some help? (Y/N)' at the bottom of the screen. Press RETURN or N, and re-type the command correctly.

Getting started

Loading the dBASE III Plus program will differ slightly with different configurations. In general, though, you will be able to follow either of the two sets of instructions here; if yours is different from either of these, make a note of the difference below for ready reference.

Using Dual Floppy Disk Drives only:

1. Switch the computer on and place dBASE System Disk 1 in drive A.
2. At the A> prompt, type DBASE and press RETURN
3. After a frew seconds, you will be instructed to:
'Insert System Disk 2 and press ENTER, or press CTRL–C to abort'.
Remove disk 1, and put system disk 2 into drive A
Press the RETURN key.
4. The copyright message appears for a few seconds, and then dBASE automatically starts by displaying the ASSIST Menu.

Press the ESC key to clear the screen and obtain the dot prompt.
At the foot of the screen you will see the following:

```
[Command Line][ <A:> ][                ][      ][    ][    ]
Enter a dBASE III Plus Command
```

Always check this display at the foot of the screen; you are usually given some guidance here by dBASE on what to do next.

The command line, or 'Status Bar', shows in reverse video the current command, data disk drive, file open, etc.
5. Place your data disk in Drive B, and enter the following command:

SET DEFAULT TO B: RETURN

Note the change in the status line below, and continue from the note below.

Using a Hard disk

1 Switch the computer on, and select the directory holding the dBASE III Plus programs.
2 At the prompt, type DBASE and press RETURN
3 The dBASE copyright notice is displayed, followed by the assist menu.
Press the ESC key to clear the screen and obtain the dot prompt as described at (4) above.
4 If you are using drive A for your data disk, place it in drive A and enter the following command:

SET DEFAULT TO A: (RETURN)

Note dBASE automatically starts at the assist menu because of the COMMAND = ASSIST entry in the system disk's CONFIG.DB file. To prevent this in future, see the 'Getting Started' booklet provided with the dBASE III Plus manual, and remove this line. You could also put the SET DEFAULT command into Config.DB to save having to do this each time you start.

If you inadvertently forget to SET the DEFAULT drive, any file you create will be saved onto the program disk instead of your data disk. If this happens, copy it over with the dBASE command:

COPY FILE <filename> TO <diskdrive:filename>

remove it from the wrong disk with the dBASE command:

ERASE <filename> – then remember to issue the SET DEFAULT To command!

Quitting dBASE III Plus

Never turn off the computer without first exiting from dBASE III Plus by means of the QUIT command. This ensures that any files that are open at this point are properly closed. If you were to finish without properly closing a file, then any alterations you were making to it at that point may not be saved.
When you are ready to leave dBASE, at the dot prompt, type:

QUIT Press RETURN

This returns you to the operating system.

Task 1

Creating a database file

Objective

To create a database file area on disk, specify the layout of each record, and print out the design specification.
Note This task does not store any data in the file.

Instructions

In the course of this training guide, you will design a very simple budget account system for a retail company, based on three database files: one to hold customer details, one to hold their transaction details, and a third to hold department headings.

For the purposes of this task, you will design the database to hold customer details. Each record will hold an account number, name, address, date of opening the account, credit limit, monthly repayment, and current balance. These are the FIELDS on each and every RECORD in the database FILE. (*See* the introduction for explanations of these terms.)

Specify the file's name at the time of creating it. This can be up to eight characters long, but make it as meaningful and as short as possible – always a good rule to follow. For each field specify a name, the type of data it will hold, and its overall width. Field names can be up to ten characters long, but again, keep them as short and as meaningful as possible.

Follow the start up instructions to get dBASE III+ loaded.

Activity 1.1

At the dot prompt, type CREATE NAMADD
Press the RETURN key to finish the command. This is the way to finish a command in dBASE, and from now on this instruction will be omitted.
Note NAMADD is the name of the database file.
dBase leaves the dot prompt mode, and displays information to help you specify the 'structure', or layout, of your NAMADD records. The cursor is in position ready to start entering details about the first field.
Note Fields are numbered to the left as you enter them; at the bottom of the screen should appear:

```
[CREATE  ][<B:>][NAMADD     ][Field: 1/1  ][    ][    ]
Enter the Field name
Field names begin with a letter and may contain letters, digits and underscores.
```

Type REF in the area under 'Field name' and press RETURN.
The cursor skips into the TYPE column, where 'Character' is already displayed. Press the space bar several times to see the different types of field possible (character, numeric, date, logical, memo). When it shows 'character' again
press RETURN to choose that type.
Character will allow any characters to be entered.
Numeric holds only numbers, including decimal point and/or sign.
Date holds only dates, two digits each for day/month/year (*See* Task 2).
Logical holds a single character T or F, or Y or N to indicate True or False.
Memo allows you to hold comparatively lengthy notes pertaining to a record, held in a memo field.

The cursor skips into the WIDTH column.
Type 4 and press **RETURN**.
This specifies that the reference number (REF) is to be four characters wide on each record. You will not be asked to specify any decimal places under DEC, and the cursor will skip to the second field line.
Complete the specification of the record layout using the information below. If you mistype, use the backspace key to erase.
(If you really make a mess of it, press **ESC** twice and start all over again from the .CREATE prompt!).

	Field name	*Type*	*Width*	*Dec*	
1	REF	character	4		
2	FIRSTNAME	character	16		
3	SURNAME	character	16		
4	TITLE	character	4		
5	OPENED	date	8		(*See* Note 1)
6	CRLIM	numeric	4	0	(*See* Note 2)
7	REPAY	numeric	6	2	
8	BAL	numeric	7	2	

Note 1 Under TYPE, press the space bar until DATE appears, then press **RETURN**. The width will automatically be set to 8 for you.
Note 2 For NUMERIC fields, specify the OVERALL width, i.e. allow for and include any decimal places, decimal point, and sign.

Check your entries. If necessary make any corrections, using the menu for help in moving the cursor, deleting, etc.
When the cursor skips to field 9, press **CTRL–END** to complete the specification.
dBASE prompts: Press **ENTER** to confirm. Any other key to resume.
Press **RETURN**.

Please wait . . . appears whilst the database structure is saved onto disk.
dBASE then prompts: Input data records now? (Y/N)
Type N to indicate that you do *not* wish to enter data now.
dBASE returns to the dot prompt:

[Command Line][<B:>][NAMADD][Rec: None][ ][ ]
Enter a dBASE III PLUS Command

To check record layout on screen, type DISPLAY STRUCTURE.
To print it out, make sure that your printer is on-line and type
DISPLAY STRUCTURE TO PRINT

Activity 1.2

Create a second database, to take the customers' transaction details. Name the file TRANS. Specify record layouts as follows:

	Field Name	*Type*	*Width*	*Dec*
1	REF	character	4	
2	REC	character	3	
3	AMOUNT	numeric	6	2
4	TDATE	date	8	
5	DEPT	character	3	

When you have finished, obtain a printout of the structure.
Note If you notice any errors in either database structure, these can be amended by using MODIFY STRUCTURE (*See* Task 6).
Either QUIT dBASE at this point, or continue to Task 2.

Key words

Task 2 Putting data into the database

Objective

To add new records to a new or existing database.

Instructions

To use a database open it with the USE command.

To insert a record, or records, use the APPEND command.

Put the customer details shown opposite into the NAMADD file specified in Task 1, inserting one record per customer (a total of seven records).

Each customer has a unique reference or account number, which is held under REF. This is the KEY FIELD, i.e. the unique identifier for that particular record, and is the first one in each record.

Activity 2.1

1 Type USE NAMADD.
2 Type APPEND.
dBASE leaves the dot prompt to go into one of its editing modes. It displays a blank 'template' in which the field names you specified in Task 1 are shown, with a highlighted area alongside each. This template enables you to enter quickly and easily the data that is required in the appropriate field areas. The cursor is in the REF area, ready for you to start entering data for the first record. Above the template is a menu to remind you how to move the cursor, delete, and complete the edit, etc.
Instructions for entering the first record's data are given here.
Type T001 in REF
(*Note* The last three characters are numbers, so enter zero-zero-one) This fills the REF field, causing the cursor to skip automatically into the NAME field area.
Type Shelagh in FIRSTNAME, then press RETURN to move the cursor onto the next field. Use upper and lower case letters as shown – what you type is what will be stored on the record in the database.
Type Thomas in SURNAME then press RETURN.
Type Mrs in TITLE and press RETURN.
Press RETURN in OPENED to leave the date blank at this point. (Do this on all seven records as you enter them).
Type 480 in CRLIM and press RETURN.
Type 20 in REPAY and press RETURN.
Type 0 in BAL and press RETURN.
Note Decimal places appear and data is justified to the right automatically when you press RETURN on these three numeric fields.
Having accepted the complete set of data for the first record, the template will clear, ready to receive the next record.
Using the customer details given below, enter the details for the remaining six records.
When the blank template appears after the last record, press RETURN once to return to the dot prompt. This will write the final records on the file and return you to the dot prompt.
Type CLEAR to clear the screen.

Data for NAMADD.DBF

REF	TITLE	F/NAME	SURNAME	CREDIT LIMIT	MONTHLY REPAYMENT
T001	Mrs	Shelagh	Thomas	480	20.00
C001	Miss	Jill	Cherry	600	25.00
T002	Mr	Grahame	Thomas	720	30.00
S001	Mr	James	Scott	480	20.00
S002	Mr	Henry	Smedley	1200	50.00
W001	Miss	Christine	Wrighton	960	40.00
M001	Mrs	Anne	Macey	600	25.00

Activity 2.2

Open the TRANS database.
Switch Caps Lock on.
Type SET DATE BRITISH.
This ensures that dates can be entered in the sequence day/month/year, in the format dd/mm/yy.
See Task 9 for more information on handling dates.
Type SET CARRY ON.
CARRY ON is a useful facility to use for entering a number of records in which some of the fields hold identical values on each. When you have completed the data entry for one record, instead of displaying a blank template for the next, it will display the values from the previous record. The purpose of using SET CARRY ON is to cut down on the amount of typing – you simply put data into the fields which are different from the previous record, and press RETURN on those which are the same. The only exception to this rule is that you cannot press RETURN to repeat the first field's contents (*see* REF in records 10,13,16,21,23, and 24) – to do so would terminate Append. (If you do this, simply type APPEND to carry on from where you left off.)
The first seven records to go onto the TRANS database are PAYMENT amounts for each customer. The REC, DATE, and DEPT are identical on each record, and all you have to enter for the second to seventh records is the REF and AMOUNT.
Similarly, most of the subsequent records are PURchase transactions made on the same dates; on these, once you have entered the details of record 8, you need only enter REF, AMOUNT, and DEPT until you get to records 15 and 17.
Insert the following records.
Note The record count increases in the command line as you go.
Take care at the end of records in which you fill the complete DEPT field with three characters (or space) – it automatically points you into the next record.

Data for TRANS.DBF

	REF	REC	AMOUNT	DATE	DEPT
1	M001	PAY	25.00	28/11/91	
2	C001	PAY	25.00	28/11/91	
3	S001	PAY	20.00	28/11/91	
4	S002	PAY	50.00	28/11/91	
5	T001	PAY	20.00	28/11/91	
6	T002	PAY	30.00	28/11/91	
7	W001	PAY	40.00	28/11/91	
8	T001	PUR	96.99	30/11/91	LF
9	W001	PUR	50.00	30/11/91	LF
10	W001	PUR	32.50	30/11/91	CF
11	M001	PUR	24.99	30/11/91	PER
12	T002	PUR	175.00	30/11/91	GF
13	T002	PUR	299.00	30/11/91	ELE
14	S002	PUR	625.00	30/11/91	LF
15	C001	PUR	127.50	01/12/91	LF
16	C001	PUR	49.00	01/12/91	TOY
17	T002	RET	–13.50	01/12/91	GF
18	S001	PUR	22.75	01/12/91	CHI
19	W001	PUR	19.99	01/12/91	TOY
20	T001	PUR	47.50	02/12/91	GF
21	T001	PUR	18.75	02/12/91	TOY
22	M001	PUR	28.50	02/12/91	CHI
23	M001	PUR	34.60	02/12/91	TOY
24	M001	PUR	55.00	02/12/91	LF

Note On record 10 *do not* press **RETURN** on REF; enter W001 again.

After the last record, press **RETURN**

Type SET CARRY OFF

CLEAR

This will discontinue the carry function, in the event of any further insertions, and clear the screen.

Quit dBASE or continue to Task 3.

Task 3

Simple information retrieval from the database

Objective

To list all, or part of, any or all records.

Instructions

Database records can be viewed quickly and simply with LIST or DISPLAY. Each of these commands may have a number of optional parameters, for specifying your particular requirements.

The format for each is:

LIST [<scope>] [<expression list>] [FOR <condition>] [OFF] [TO PRINT]
DISPLAY

Scope defines the number of records to be listed. If omitted from LIST it is assumed to be ALL, and dBASE starts at the first record. If omitted from DISPLAY it is assumed to be only the next (or current) record.

Expression list defines what is to be shown from each record in the list. If omitted, all fields will be displayed. An expression can be a field or a formula performing some sort of calculation on fields.

For can be used to select specific records for the list/display. Unless you specify a NEXT scope, dBase will search the whole file for records meeting your specification.

Off prohibits the printing of record numbers on the left.

To print will direct the output to the printer as well as to the screen. If omitted, output will be displayed on screen only. Check that your printer is on-line first.

Activity

Carry out the following LIST and DISPLAY commands, noting for each the effect of including different parameters.

Open your database file USE TRANS

No parameters at all:

Type DISPLAY

Type LIST

Type GO TOP

This points you back to the first record in the file. From now on, notice that the position of the RECORD POINTER is shown in the command line at the bottom of the screen.

Using the scope parameter:

Type	LIST NEXT 3	
	DISPLAY RECORD 5	to view the fifth record on file.
	DISPLAY NEXT 2	to view the 5th and 6th records
	DISPLAY ALL	to list all records on file. Unlike LIST on its own, this allows you to read a screenful at a time – at your own pace.
Type	GO TOP	

Using expression list parameters:

Open the NAMADD file and type DISPLAY REF,FIRSTNAME,SURNAME
LIST REF, CRLIM, REPAY, CRLIM/REPAY
GO TOP

Using scope and expression list:

Type LIST NEXT 3 TITLE, SURNAME, REPAY
DISPLAY NEXT 2 REF, SURNAME, CRLIM

Using the FOR < condition > parameter:
To list records in which the customer's credit limit is 480, type
DISPLAY FOR CRLIM = 480
To list all customers whose monthly repayment is less than £30, type
LIST REF,FIRSTNAME,SURNAME,REPAY FOR REPAY < 30
The scope is assumed to be ALL whenever a FOR condition is specified and no scope is specified.
More than one condition can be given. To list the references and firstnames of customers whose surname is Thomas and whose credit limit is more than £500: type
LIST FOR CRLIM > 500 .AND. SURNAME = "Thomas"
Note 1 Quotation marks are required around characters being compared with any non-numeric field.
Note 2 A full stop is required either side of the logical operators AND and OR joining two conditions.
Note 3 Relational operator symbols to use are:

= Equal	<> or Not Equal	< Less than
> More than	> = More than or equal	< = Less than or equal

Using all three parameters:
Type GO TOP
DISPLAY NEXT 3 REF,TITLE,SURNAME FOR CRLIM > 500

Using the OFF and TO PRINT parameters:

So far, records have been displayed on the screen, with a record number border.
Add the parameter OFF to remove this, e.g. LIST REF, SURNAME, BAL, CRLIM OFF
To print out on paper, use similar LIST and DISPLAY commands with TO PRINT as the final parameter, e.g. LIST REF, TITLE, FIRSTNAME, SURNAME OFF TO PRINT
Make sure that your printer is ready, and try all the above commands again, this time adding either TO PRINT, or OFF, or both of them.
Note At the end of a list of display instruction to the printer, the final line is held in a memory buffer area: press the on-line printer switch to print this line.

Key words

Display 1, 6, 8, 9, 11, 18
Expression
For 4, 5, 10, 16
Go/Goto
List 7, 9, 18, 25
Off
Parameters 23
Scope 4, 5
Skip 7
To print 1
Use 2, 11

Task 4 Keeping the database up-to-date

Objective

To alter contents of current records.

Instructions

EDIT allows you to alter the contents of any record(s) in the database, dealing with them one record at a time on screen.

Typing EDIT on its own will assume that editing is to start at the current record, so if your record pointer is currently at record number 6, that is the one that would be presented for editing. EDIT displays a data entry screen like the one used to insert the new records in Activity 2.1. To make changes to the contents of any field, move the cursor to the required position and then delete, insert, or overwrite as required. Use the arrow keys for cursor movement.

Note the menu at the top guides you, i.e.:

CTRL–G deletes a character.

CTRL–Y deletes an entire field.

CTRL–U marks the current record for DELETION – Task 5 will deal with deleting records.

INS (or CTRL–V) allows you to INSERT characters (rather than overwrite what is there already, which is otherwise assumed). When you set Insert ON, INS appears in the command line.

INS a second time will switch the INSERT mode off.

The PGDN key moves the cursor onto the next record.

The PGUP key moves the cursor back to the previous record.

CTRL–W or CTRL–END writes the existing record and returns to the dot prompt.

RETURN moves the cursor onto the next field.

Activity 4.1

Open the database NAMADD

Type EDIT

Use the cursor arrow keys to move the cursor into and along the FIRSTNAME field, and change the name there to Shelagh M.

Press the PGDN key twice to move onto G Thomas' record.

Delete the letter E at the end of the first name, so that it reads 'Graham'.

Exit from the EDIT mode and write the altered database back to disk by pressing CTRL–END

If you had pressed ESC to finish off, the last edit would not have been saved.

To edit a specific record:

Type EDIT 7.

This would present the seventh (Anne Macey's) record. Alter the TITLE to Ms, and then end the Edit.

Instructions

BROWSE differs from EDIT only in the way that the records are displayed on screen. It presents them horizontally, one screen at a time. All fields will be displayed unless you use the FIELDS parameter to limit them. Record numbers are not shown on each line, but the current record number is always shown in the command line below.

Activity 4.2

Open the TRANS database, and type BROWSE
Move the cursor down to the fifth record using the DOWN arrow key, and then along to the AMOUNT field using the END key. (*See* the menu above). Alter the AMOUNT to 40.00.
Examine this record list and correct any mistakes that might have been made when creating the file earlier. Use the PGDN key to display the next screen.
Complete the Browse with CTRL–END

Instructions

GLOBAL EDITING with REPLACE
Format: REPLACE [<scope>] <field> WITH <expression> [FOR <condition>]
The REPLACE command is useful when you want to alter the same field(s) on several or all records.

Activity 4.3

Open the database NAMADD
Type REPLACE ALL opened WITH CTOD("28/11/91")
Note The meaning of CTOD() around the date, and the way that dBase deals with dates generally, are explained in Task 9.
Type REPLACE ALL CRLIM WITH CRLIM*1.10 This will increase everyone's credit limit by ten per cent.
Arithmetic signs are: + plus, – minus, * multiply, / divide.
Type REPLACE ALL BAL WITH CRLIM/2
This will set everyone's balance to half the credit limit (for the purpose of these tasks).
List the contents of NAMADD to see that every record now has an opened date of 28/11/88, and an increased credit limit.
Quit dBASE

Key words

Task 5 Deleting records

Objective To delete whole records from a database.

Instructions

Deleting a record in dBASE is a two-step process: first mark the records for deletion, then remove them from the database by 'packing' the file.

The first step can be achieved by *either* using the CTRL–U function in EDIT or BROWSE mode *or* using the DELETE command at the dot prompt.

Before deleting any records, make a copy of the database as it now stands, so that you can get back to the same point at the end of this activity.

Neither file in a copy must be open already; if TRANS is in use from Task 4, type USE first. USE on its own will close a database. Then, at the dot prompt, type
COPY FILE trans.dbf TO trans.cop

This will create a back-up copy of the database on the same disk, calling it TRANS.COP, and will display 1024 BYTES COPIED before returning to the dot prompt.

Activity 5.1

Deleting records using EDIT
Open database TRANS and edit record 10.
When this record is displayed, look at the menu above, and find the DELETE section.
When the prompt 'Record: ^U' appears, press CTRL–U to mark the record for deletion.
Note At the bottom of the screen, DEL will appear in the right-hand corner of the command line. This indicates that this record has been marked for deletion.
CTRL–U is what is called a 'toggle', i.e. it can be used and reused to do and undo the same action. If you press CTRL–U again now the DEL will disappear and the record will be unmarked. A third CTRL–U will mark it again, and so on.
Delete records 10 and 14, then display the whole file to see the effect.

Activity 5.2

Deleting records using BROWSE

If you have several records to delete it can be quicker to use BROWSE. Go back to the beginning of TRANS and use the BROWSE command to edit the database. CTRL–U is used in the same way with Browse. Mark the 16th to 20th (inclusive) records for deletion, then finish the BROWSE operation.

Instructions

Deleting records using DELETE

The DELETE command can be issued on its own to delete the current record only. It can also be used with the SCOPE and/or FOR <condition> parameters, for example:

DELETE	delete the current record.
DELETE RECORD 22	deletes record 22.
DELETE NEXT 3	deletes the next 3 records starting with the current record.

DELETE ALL FOR REC = "PAY"
deletes all records with "PAY" in the REC field.

DELETE ALL deletes every record.

Activity 5.3

Open the TRANS database and delete all the PAYMENT records.
Display the whole file, to check that the correct records have been marked. Records marked for deletion will have an asterisk (*) alongside each customer's reference. It is always wise to check that only the correct records have been marked, before completing the record deletion operation. If any are wrongly marked, either alter them using BROWSE or EDIT, or use the RECALL command. RECALL reinstates the current record, but if used with the SCOPE or FOR parameters, can be made to restore all or several records.
Type RECALL FOR REC = "PAY"
DISPLAY FOR REC = "PAY"

Instructions

Completing the deletion operation

Whichever method you use to mark records to be deleted, they will be removed permanently from the database by the PACK command. Once this has been done, you cannot get them back, unless you have taken a security copy beforehand. Make sure that you always check the file and make any necessary changes before using PACK.

Activity 5.4

Type PACK
Display the whole file again to verify that records marked have disappeared from the file.
To save typing all the data in again, recover from the back-up copy TRANS.COP.
Type USE. This will close the database, so that you can copy back onto it.
Type COPY FILE trans.cop TO trans.dbf
A warning message asks: 'TRANS.DBF already exists, overwrite it? (Y/N)'. Type Y (To overwrite the current version of the file).
This will restore the database to what it was at the beginning of Task 5.
Open it up and list its contents to prove it for yourself.
Quit dBASE or continue to the next task.

Key words

Task 6

Altering record layouts

Objective

To use MODIFY STRUCTURE and note its effect on a file already containing data records.

Instructions

When you enter MODIFY STRUCTURE, dBASE leaves the dot prompt mode, and displays a screen similar to that used in Task 1 when creating the file. The fields already defined then are shown, with the cursor positioned in the first.

The arrow, insert, and delete keys are used in just the same way. The records in the NAMADD database each contain eight fields, which were specified with the CREATE command in Task 1. Alter the records to include the address details.

Activity 6.1

Open the NAMADD database.
Type MODIFY STRUCTURE.
Move the cursor down to field number 5 (OPENED), and insert the following fields, pressing CTRL–N before each one (*see* the menu above to confirm this).

Fieldname	*Type*	*Width*	*Dec*
LINE1	Character	20	
LINE2	Character	20	
LINE3	Character	20	
POSTCODE	Character	10	

Using the menu displayed at the top of the screen, look in the right-hand section for the Exit/Save option.
Press CTRL–END
dBASE will request: Press ENTER to confirm, any other key to resume
Press RETURN
Print out a hard copy of the new record structure.
Type DISPLAY ALL
Note Each record still holds the same data intact, but now has four extra empty fields, bringing the total record size to 136 characters (bytes). This is clearly too wide to fit on one line, and so each record spills over two lines. It is when records are large like this that specifying particular fields, in a list or display, can be useful.

Activity 6.2 Update (EDIT) the whole file with the following address details, pressing PGDN to move through the file (*Note* Each record now requires two screens to display its complete list of fields).

REF	ADDRESS			POST CODE
T001	5 Oaktree Lane	Oakley	AYLESBURY, Bucks	HP18 9KJ
C001	6 Ullswater Park	BELFAST	N Ireland	BT8 9GZ
T002	40 Northfield Ave	Westbury-on-Trym	BRISTOL	BS6 3FD
S001	Creag Dhu	Rosehall	LAIRG, Sutherland	LS12 3NB
S002	71 Guildford Ave	BLACKPOOL	Fylde	FY30 6GB
W00	5 Field Close	LLANDUDNO	Gwynedd	LL6 5RQ
M00	5 St Mary's Close	PUTNEY	LONDON	SW16 8JN

List these fields on the printer.

Key words

Display 1, 3, 8, 9, 11, 18
Edit 2, 4, 5, 12, 13, 17
Modify 12, 16, 17, 18, 21, 27

Task 7

Useful tips, commands and features

Objective

To try out useful commands, which can be used when required in succeeding tasks.

Instructions

To speed up command entry

Dot prompt commands have been shown in this guide written in full. They can be entered in an abbreviated form by using just the first four letters; for example, you may enter DISPLAY as DISP. Try this out in the following activities.

Note commands will continue to be shown in full throughout this text.

Another useful feature is the way dBASE keeps a 'history' of the commands you have been entering. Unless you tell it otherwise, the last twenty commands are stored in memory, and you can review and repeat any of them by pressing the upward arrow key. The commands appear on the dot prompt line as you move backwards (or forwards) through them. When you reach the command you intend to repeat, either press RETURN or, if you want to alter it first, move along the command entry line to wherever you wish to insert or overwrite the character(s), make the change and then press RETURN. For example, to display records on the screen and then print out the same information. Press the up arrow to get the display command at the prompt again, move the cursor along the line (CTRL–F is quickest) and add TO PRINT on the end.

You will be reminded of this in the exercise which follows. To list or display the commands you have issued type

LIST HISTORY [> TO PRINT <]

Activity 7.1

To set print on/off

If can be useful to keep a printout of your work as you do it. Type SET PRINT ON to print out everything, commands and output. To stop it, type SET PRINT OFF

Make sure that your printer is on-line.

Type SET PRINT ON and leave it on for the following activities.

Instructions

To move the record pointer

You have already used GO TOP to move back to the start of an open database.

There are also:

GO BOTTOM	moves to the last record
GOTO <n>	moves to the nth record
SKIP <n>	moves forward n records, (default one record)

Activity 7.2 Use the following commands, and note the position of the record pointer in the command status line below.

Type USE TRANS
DISP [For each DISPLAY, use the up arrow key to get the
DISP NEXT 4 previous one and press RETURN]
SKIP
DISP
SKIP 3
DISP
GO TOP
DISP
GO BOTTOM
DISP

Instructions To locate a particular record.

LOCATE is used to find a particular record, displaying the record number when found, or 'End of LOCATE scope' if no match can be found. The format is:
LOCATE FOR <condition>

Activity 7.3 To look up the record of a customer whose surname is Thomas, but you are not sure which one, type USE NAMADD
LOCA FOR surname = 'Thomas'
DISP

To locate the next and any other Thomas' records, rather than retype the full LOCATE command again, repeat the CONTINUE command, until the 'End of Locate' is reached.

Type CONTINUE
DISPLAY [Finds Record 3]
CONT [Reaches "End of LOCATE scope"]

Type SET PRINT OFF to terminate printing everything out.

Instructions To compare character fields and strings successfully.

To find a match in the LOCATE above, you had to type in the name THOMAS using upper and lower case letters exactly as they had been used to enter the name in the database. This can be awkward if you are not sure how the field contents have been entered.

Activity 7.4

Type LOCATE FOR SURNAME = "THOMAS"
LOCA FOR REF = "w001"

Both of these result in the 'End of LOCATE scope' message without any records having been located. This problem can be overcome by telling dBASE to convert the contents to upper case letters for the purpose of comparison only.

Type LOCA FOR UPPER(SURNAME) = "THOMAS"
LOCA FOR REF = UPPER("w001")

This time each LOCATE succeeds in finding a record.

You need only give the first few characters of a string, if this is sufficient to identify what you are looking for.
Type LOCATE FOR UPPER(SURNAME) = "THOM"
Note This would also find a record for Thomson, Thomason, etc if such records were on file.
Finally, quit dBASE, or continue to the next task.

Key words

Task 8 Further information retrieval

Objective

To extract totals and averages; to count records; to use memory as an interim work area in these or other operations.

Activity 8.1

Format: COUNT [FOR <condition>] [TO memvar>]

To find out how many records you have on file use COUNT.
Type USE TRANS
COUNT
"24 Records" is displayed before the next dot prompt.
To find out how many records satisfy a given condition, e.g. how many purchase records there are, use COUNT FOR <condition>
Type COUNT FOR rec = "PAY"
"7 records" is then displayed.

Activity 8.2

Format AVERAGE <expression> [FOR <condition>] [TO <memvar>]

This is used to find the average of a numeric field or expression, e.g. the average agreed monthly
repayment value can be obtained by typing USE NAMADD
AVERAGE REPAY
The following is then displayed:
7 records averaged
Average Repay
30.00
To obtain the average difference between credit limit (CRLIM) and actual current balance (BAL), type:
AVERAGE CRLIM – BAL
To obtain the average purchase value, type:
USE TRANS
AVERAGE amount FOR rec = "PUR"

Activity 8.3

Format: SUM <expression> [FOR <condition>] [TO <memvar>]

To get the total of a numeric field(s), use the SUM command:
Type USE TRANS
SUM AMOUNT
The number of records and total amount will be displayed.

Instructions

In the last three commands, you will have noticed an extra parameter, [TO <memvar<]. 'Memvar' is short for Memory Variable, and refers to an area outside the database, in RAM, where you can store something for later reference.

It can be regarded as a field in which you can temporarily store numbers, or characters, or a date.

Activity 8.4

Type USE TRANS
COUNT FOR rec = "PAY" TO PAYTOT
COUNT FOR rec = "RET" TO RTOT
SUM AMOUNT FOR REF = "T002" .AND. REC = "PUR" TO T002TOT

Instructions

The contents of memory variables can be examined by means of the DISPLAY MEMORY command. This will show the name, type, and contents of each memory variable currently in use.

A variable is created when you first use it in the TO <memvar> parameter in a command.

Activity 8.5

To place an initial value of your own, or the result of an expression, into memory, use the STORE command.
STORE <expression> TO <memvar>
Type STORE 150 TO MVA
STORE 123*4/3 TO MVB
STORE "Example 1" TO MVC
GO TOP
STORE ref TO MVD
DISPLAY MEMORY
Now enter
STORE 876 TO MVA
STORE "Example 2" TO MVC
to overwrite the previous contents of MVA and MVC, and not create further variables.
Type DISPLAY MEMORY again to prove it.
A variable becomes a certain type of field according to what you put into it when creating it for the first time. Thereafter, you can only overwrite its contents with data of the same type. You cannot, for example, now type: STORE "Example 3" TO MVA, because MVA is a numeric field.
Quit dBASE or continue to the next task.

Key words

Accept
Average
Count
Display 1, 3, 6, 9, 11, 18
Field type 1, 2
Memory variables
Store 20
Sum

Task 9 **Dates**

Objective To learn how dBASE III Plus handles dates

Instructions Dates can be entered and displayed by dBASE III Plus in any of the following formats:

American:	mm/dd/yy	**British** or **French**:	dd/mm/yy
Ansi:	yy.mm.dd	**Italian**:	dd-mm-yy
German:	dd.mm.yy		

American format is assumed unless you specify otherwise. For example, when you created the TRANS and NAMADD databases, you defined certain fields as being of DATE type. Before you set about entering record details, you were instructed to use the SET DATE BRITISH command. Had you not done this, you would have had to enter the dates in American format.

Once you have issued the SET DATE command it remains in force until you quit dBASE or until you use it again.

Activity 9.1 Open the TRANS database and list the reference, date and amount from each record.
Dates appear in American mm/dd/yy format.

Open the NAMADD file. Edit Record 1, making the OPENED date field 30 November 1991. Try to enter this as 30/11/91 and press RETURN; you will get the message: Invalid date. (press SPACE) and the cursor will still be on the OPENED line. Press the space bar, and re-enter the date, this time with month first: 11/30/88.
As soon as you have entered this, the cursor moves onto the next field (leaving the 'Invalid' message on screen). Press CTRL–END to get back to the dot prompt.

Type SET DATE BRITISH
The effect of this is two-fold: dates will be displayed; and you can enter them, in the format dd/mm/yy.
Alter the dates on the first two records, setting OPENED to 27 November.

Instructions Date functions DTOC() and CTOD()

A function is not a dBASE Command – it is used with commands. Both date functions DTOC() and CTOD() are used to convert data types; date to character, or character to date respectively. They can be used in a number of commands which use dates, but are particularly useful when you wish to compare or replace a date-type field with a character string. This is because in any comparison or replacement, the two data items involved must be of the *same* type.

When you specify a literal, it will be either a numeric value, or a character string within quotes, e.g.:

DISPLAY FOR CRLIM > 1000	(where 1000 is numeric)
LIST SURNAME FOR REF = "C001"	(where C001 is character type)

Activity 9.2

To match a date-type field with a character string, convert the date-type to character.
Type LIST REF,SURNAME,OPENED FOR OPENED = "28/11/91"
This results in: "Data type mismatch".
"Do you want some help? (Y/N)"
Press RETURN.
Type DISP REF,SURNAME FOR DTOC(opened) = "28/11/91"
Alternatively, convert the character string to date-type as follows:
Type DISP REF,SURNAME FOR opened = CTOD("30/11/91")
Note This requirement for converting to/from characters/dates is required with any commands where there is likely to be a 'mis-match' – e.g., when updating a date field: REPLACE OPENED WITH "28/11/91" would result in the error 'Data type mis-match', whereas REPLACE OPENED WITH CTOD("28/11/91") would work.
Set print ON and open the TRANS database.
For each of the following, display the Ref,Rec,Amount:
All records with TDATE of 28 November 1991 (= Records 1 – 7)
All purchases after 30 November 1991 (Records 15 – 24)

Activity 9.3

Other date functions

To obtain the current system date, use DATE() as a parameter to other commands. (*See* Task 7 for useful tips)

```
STORE DATE() TO today
STORE DATE()–1 TO yester
STORE DATE()+30 TO nextmnth
USE TRANS
STORE TDATE TO mdate
REPLACE TDATE WITH DATE()
DISPLAY
REPLACE TDATE WITH DATE()–4
DISPLAY
REPLACE TDATE WITH TDATE+3
DISPLAY
REPLACE TDATE WITH MDATE
```

Instructions

Note It is easy to add or subtract a number of days from a date field. This facility could be useful, for example, when you want to set a pay-by date for customers 30 days from the date of invoice.
To obtain the weekday name from a date, use CDOW(<date variable>)
To obtain the month name from a date, use CMONTH(<date variable>)
To obtain the day (of the month) number from a date, use DAY(<date variable>)
To obtain the day of the week number (Sunday is day 1) from a date, use DOW(<date variable>)
To obtain the month number from a date, use MONTH(<date variable>)
To obtain the four-digit year from a date, use YEAR(<date variable>)

Activity 9.4 Try the following:

```
USE TRANS
DISPLAY CDOW(tdate)
DISPLAY CMONTH(tdate)
DISPLAY FOR DAY(tdate) = 1
GO TOP
DISPLAY ALL DOW(tdate) FOR REC = "PUR" .AND. DEPT = "TOY"
GO TOP
DISPLAY MONTH(tdate)
DISPLAY YEAR(DATE())
DISPLAY CMONTH(DATE))
DISPLAY CDOW(DATE())
DISP CDOW(DATE()) + "," + CMONTH(DATE()) + " " + ; LTRIM(STR(DAY(DATE())),2))
  + ", "+ STR(YEAR(DATE()),4) RETURN

SET PRINT OFF
```

Key words

Cdow
Cmonth 18
Ctod
Dates 1, 2
Display 1, 3, 6, 8, 11, 18
Dtoc 11
Function 7, 15, 16, 28
Replace 4, 19
Set date 2

Task 10 Sorting

Objective

To rearrange the sequence of records onto a second database, leaving the original database unchanged.

Instructions

Format:
SORT <scope> TO <newfile> ON <fieldname>[/D] [,<field2> [/D]] [FOR <condition>]

Two parameters are needed for SORT : the name of the database on which the sorted records are to be stored, and the field(s) which are to act as the sort key. It does not matter which you specify first, but the /D parameter, if used, must always follow its fieldname.

Sort your file as often as you wish, but each time you will create a new database (or overwrite an existing one).

Always sort from the original database (NAMADD or TRANS) onto the same two copies (NAMADD2 or TRANS2).

Activity 10.1

Type USE NAMADD
SORT TO NAMADD2 ON SURNAME
"100% Sorted 7 records sorted is displayed

Close NAMADD and open the sorted database that you have just created.

Type USE NAMADD2
DISPLAY ALL REF,SURNAME,OPENED,CRLIM

Open the TRANS database and sort it into REFerence number sequence onto a file called TRANS2. Print out the whole file in this new sequence.
Open the TRANS database and sort it into DEPT descending sequence, onto TRANS2 again. Add the extra parameter /D after the fieldname to indicate a descending sequence. This time, before carrying out the sort, dBASE will ask:
TRANS2.dbf already exists, overwrite it? (Y/N)
Type Y
Print out the new file.
Sort and print out the reference, title and both names of customers in order of surname and firstname.
Note After this sort, your two customers whose surname is Thomas are listed alphabetically, not in reference, sequence. When specifying more than one sort key field, name them, in order of priority, together separated by a comma, e.g. ON SURNAME,FIRSTNAME.
Sort and print out the full names and credit limits of customers in descending order of credit limit, with names listed alphabetically for each credit limit value.
Sort and print out the amount and department for all purchases, in departmental sequence.
At this point, you will have four database files in your directory. Confirm this as follows: Type DIR. This will list the database files, giving for each, the filename, the number of records held in the file, the date it was last updated, and its file storage size.

Note It is important to remember that the file you have open when you use SORT remains in its own same sequence. To use the information in the new sequence, open the new file.
Always use the original file (in our examples, NAMADD or TRANS) for all updating, and re-sort it onto the sorted database file area (overwriting) each time you need to use it in the other sequence.
A disadvantage of SORT is that a lot of disk storage space can quickly be used up, as whole new databases are created by it. The alternative is to use indexing, which is explained in the following task.

Key words	**Databases 1, 2, 11, 25** **Dir** **Field 1, 2, 4** **For 3, 4, 5, 16** **Key field 2** **Record 1, 2, 4** **Sort 11**

Task 11 Indexing

Objective

To create and use indexes with a database.

Instructions

When you used the SORT command to sort the database, it produced a second file in the required sequence, leaving the database in use unchanged.

INDEX does not create another database, nor does it sort the database itself, but creates a small separate index file. This is recognised by the characters .NDX which dBASE appends to the name you give.

Activity 11.1

Creating and using indexes

Set Print ON to record the first part of the exercise.
Type USE NAMADD
INDEX ON ref TO REFI
dBASE reports: 100% indexed 7 Records indexed.
This will create an index file for the database NAMADD called REFI.NDX. The index file will hold a list of all the REFs in ascending order with, for each, its corresponding record number in the database. This is used by dBASE to access each record in the database, in the same way that you would use the index at the back of a book to enable you to go directly to a page containing the topic you required.
An index can be used to look at the database in a particular order, so the file will appear to be sorted.
Continuing the example above, note the record numbers when you type
DISPLAY ALL ref, title, firstname, surname, crlim
SET PRINT OFF

Instructions

Having created the index file REFI.NDX on disk, it is available to use again at a future date by typing USE NAMADD INDEX REFI
This will open NAMADD and REFI.NDX, and NAMADD will appear to be sorted into REF sequence as a result.
You can create as many index files as you like, for example, to access records, either alphabetically, or in reference number order, and so on.

Activity 11.2

Open the NAMADD database and index it on POSTCODE to an index file called PC, then list all customers, showing Title Surname Line1 and Postcode, in postcode sequence.

Activity 11.3

Open the TRANS database, index it on REF to an index file called TREFI, and print out all transactions in reference order.

Instructions

More than one key field can be specified, joined together in the INDEX command by the plus (+) sign. They must all be of, or converted to, the SAME data TYPE. Indexing on REF and TDATE for instance would require you to convert the date to a character string in the INDEX command. To look at the transactions for each customer in chronological sequence: the easiest way to ensure that dates are sorted or indexed into the correct sequence is to set the date to ANSI format first:

Activity 11.4

Type SET DATE ANSI
USE TRANS
INDEX ON ref+DTOC(tdate) TO TRD
SET DATE BRITISH
DISP ALL

Activity 11.5

Open TRANS and index it chronologically, with references in sequence for each date. Name the index file TDR. Print out the file in this new sequence.

Instructions

Indexes can also speed up the search for a particular record. LOCATE was used earlier for searching for a selected record, but this carries out the search by reading through every record one by one, checking each to see if it is the one required. This should not be used when you are using an index with the database, as it could slow the processing down considerably. Instead, use the FIND command, for which the format is FIND <character string or number>.

Quotation mark delimiters are not needed around the character string, unless the key field contains leading spaces.

FIND searches for a particular record in a database by reading the index file to find the record's location.

Activity 11.6

Open NAMADD with the index REFI.
Note that the record pointer shows that record number 2 is the first record accessed via the index when it is first opened.
Type FIND T
DISP
The record pointer moves to the first record in which the index keyfield (REF) starts with 'T'.
Find and display the record with REF = S002

Instructions

Keeping indexes up-to-date

When you create more than one index for the same database, you can open them all together, by typing:

USE NAMADD INDEX REFI,PC.

The first index file named is the one which will be put into use with the USE statement. In the example above, NAMADD records will be presented as though indexed on REF, as REFI is the first named index file in the USE statement.

The point of opening *all* index files is that any updating on the database, which might affect its sequence (e.g. inserting or deleting records) would also update the index files.

If, however, the index files are not open at the time of carrying out such updates, you will have to re-index the database later. This is not necessarily a bad thing; in fact it might be better always to open the main database without indexes to do all updating and to re-index afterwards.

To illustrate this, carry out the following:

Activity 11.7

Open the NAMADD database without indexes. Insert two new customers' records, with REF B014 and C006 respectively. Each opened their accounts on 4th December, with a credit limit of £700, a monthly repayment of £50, and a zero balance. (Make up the other details yourself).

Then display Ref, name and opening date from the whole file to show the database in its original (and actual) order, with the two new records at the end of the file.

Type SET INDEX TO REFI

DISP ALL

This shows the database in REF order, but with the two new records apparently missing. This is because the index file that is now open was not in use with the database at the time of the APPEND update, and so it was not updated at the same time. The indexes can be brought up-to-date, as follows:

Type USE NAMADD INDEX REFI, PC

REINDEX

DISP ALL REF, SURNAME, POSTCODE, OPENED

SET INDEX TO PC

DISP ALL REF, SURNAME, POSTCODE, OPENED

Quit dBASE, or type CLOSE ALL before continuing to the next task.

CLOSE ALL will close all files of all types.

Key words

Task 12 Designing and printing a report

Objective

To design the layout of a report and store the specification on disk for future use.

Instructions

Commands such as List, Display and Browse are ideal for instant access to information in a database. Their style of output, however, is less than ideal. With the REPORT facility, you can specify your own page headings, the layout of each page, and optional totals or subtotals at the end.

CREATE (or MODIFY) REPORT is used to specify your report details, which are then stored on disk, in a file with .FRM appended to its name. This form file is then available for later use.

Modify can be used to create a new, or alter an existing report format.

Create is only used when specifying a new format file for the first time.

For specifying or altering a report layout, dBASE III Plus provides a series of 'pull-down' menus. From these you can enter the editing mode in order to type in headings and titles.

To illustrate this process, design a report to print customers' names and addresses.

Activity 12.1

To specify the report layout

Open the NAMADD database, then type MODIFY REPORT NAREP1
The screen will immediately change, and display the following: the menu bar across the top – with OPTIONS highlighted, the Options pull-down Menu – in which PAGE TITLE is highlighted, the cursor control, delete/insert help menu, the status bar, now showing the file NAREP1.FRM open, and two prompt lines at the foot of the screen guiding you on what to do next.
Use the arrow keys to move the highlight across the menu bar selections: Options, Groups, Columns, Locate, and Exit.
You will see that each has its own pull-down menu. The arrow keys are used for moving the highlight across, up, and down menu selections. From this point on, make a selection by highlighting your choice, and then pressing RETURN
Follow these steps carefully. If at any point you press or forget to press a key, which causes dBASE to react unexpectedly, go back to the previous option pull-down menu using the arrow keys, and restart from that point. If you get into real difficulty, start the whole activity again from the beginning.
Highlight and select OPTIONS.
Use this menu to specify page headings, overall page dimensions and some print requirements. Each option already has a default value. Enter the page title lines, alter the left margin and the page eject parameters:
PAGE TITLE will already have been selected when you press RETURN for options.
An arrow in the data entry area indicates that you have selected this option, and are now in the data entry mode. This means, as the prompt below says, that you can enter up to four lines of wording to appear at the top of each page in your report.
You are not limited to the width shown; they can each be up to 59 characters. Type
CUSTOMERS' NAME AND ADDRESS DETAILS   REF: NAREP1
Press RETURN
Press CTRL–END to complete the edit mode.

In any database system, you will probably want several different reports. It is useful to make sure that each has a unique reference as well as its title at the top of each page, and if the report is produced frequently, to have the current date shown. In this example (and those which follow) the reference will be the name of the report form file.

Highlight and select LEFT MARGIN, and alter this from 8 to 3.

Highlight and select PAGE EJECT BEFORE. This is set to YES. To alter it to NO, press RETURN once. Yes/No entries can be reversed by pressing RETURN

This completes the section dealing with overall page specification. Press the right-arrow key twice to highlight COLUMNS in the menu bar above.

Select COLUMNS to specify what is to appear in the main body of the report. Each column may hold one or more fields from the open database, or the results of some expression (e.g. subtracting one field from another).

As you specify the contents of each column, a report format template is gradually drawn and displayed below. The >>> characters indicate the width of the left margin area. *Note* This was changed from the default 8, to 3 in the OPTIONS menu.

CONTENTS will automatically have been selected when you pressed RETURN at COLUMNS.

The prompt tells you to specify the contents of Column 1 (*see* the status bar below).

Press the F10 for a list of fieldnames, select the required fieldname (REF) from the list displayed, and press RETURN again.

Highlight and select HEADING.

Up to four lines can be used for column headings; use just two, again going into data entry editing mode to do so:

Type Ref and press RETURN
No. and press RETURN

Press CTRL–END to complete the edit.

Press the PGDN key, to start specifying Column 2 (*Note* what is happending in the status bar and report template below).

Select CONTENTS

As an alternative to using the F10 help menu to specify column contents, you can just type in fieldnames.

Type FIRSTNAME+SURNAME and press RETURN

The plus (+) sign is used to join more than one field. In column 2 the whole name, comprising two fields, will be shown. dBASE III Plus automatically works out the column width.

Select HEADING

Type: Customer's Name

Press CTRL–END

Press the PGDN key to continue onto column 3's specification.

Select CONTENTS and specify as: LINE1+LINE2+LINE3

Select HEADING and specify it as: Address

Select WIDTH, and alter this to 20

Each of the three fields making up the address is 20 characters long, as they were defined in Task 6, so the width of column 3 should take up 60 characters, i.e. most of the line. Setting the width to only 20 causes dBASE to automatically print 20 characters per line within the column over as many lines as are needed to print the entire contents as specified. In other words this forces it to print three lines of address for each customer.

Press RETURN then PGDN to continue to column 4.
Select CONTENTS and specify as : POSTCODE
Select HEADING and specify as : Post Code
Press CTRL–END
The specification is now complete. Highlight the EXIT option in the menu bar, and note that SAVE is already highlighted. Press RETURN
The form file NAREP1.FRM is now stored on disk, and available for you to use.

Activity 12.2 Using the report form

Printing or displaying information from a database using a report form file is achieved with the command
REPORT FORM <format filename> [HEADING<character string>] [<FOR condition>] [TO PRINT]
The scope is assumed to be ALL.
Ensure that your printer is online, then type REPORT FORM narep1 TO PRINT
Note the function of the extra HEADING parameter in the following:
REPORT FORM NAREP1 HEADING"FEMALE ACCOUNT HOLDERS" FOR .NOT. title = "Mr "TO PRINT RETURN
REPORT FORM narep1 HEADING "Customers with Credit limit over 600" FOR crlim > 600 TO PRINT RETURN

Activity 12.3 Using the above instructions as a guide, design and use a report showing both names in Col 1, opened date in Col 2, credit limit in Col 3, and Balance in Col 4 for all customers. Give the report a reference of NAREP2 and the title 'Customer Accounts Current Status Summary'.

Key words

Task 13 Report totals

Objective

To design and use a report form which includes totals and sub-totals.

Instructions

In the previous task, you designed two reports, which in effect were a straightforward list of data from the name and address file. Create a report form for listing the transactions in the TRANS database, giving a subtotal of AMOUNT for each customer, and an overall file total at the end.

Any column containing numeric data will automatically be totalled, unless you specify NO to the TOTAL THIS COLUMN option in the columns pull-down menu.

To get sub-totals within the body of the report, use the GROUPS option to specify the group of records for which we require them. Whenever you use this option, the database has to be indexed or sorted to match this grouping. For example, to print out all the transactions for each customer with a sub-total at the end, all the records for any one customer must be grouped and accessed together. This can be achieved by using the index TREFI when opening the database, or by using a sorted version of it.

Activity 13

Open the TRANS database with the index file TREFI.
Create a report form file named TRANREP1, with the options:
Page Title: CUSTOMER TRANSACTIONS REF: TRANREP1
Page width: 76
Left margin: 18
No page ejection before printing.
Select GROUPS from the menu bar.
Set the GROUP ON EXPRESSION option to REF.
This means that sub-totals of numeric fields should be accumulated from all records until a change of REF is encountered, at which point it should be printed out.
Set the GROUP HEADING to: Account Number:
Select COLUMNS from the menu bar and specify the following :

	CONTENTS	HEADING
Col 1	Ref	Account Ref'ce
Col 2	Rec	Transaction
Col 3	Tdate	Date
Col 4	Amount	Value

Note 1 The value of TOTAL THIS COLUMN after specifying column 4's contents as amount: dBASE automatically sets this to YES for numeric fields, so you would only have to alter it if you did not want totals for this particular column.
Note 2 Widths and other parameters take the default values.
Select the EXIT option from the menu bar and save TRANREP1.FRM on disk.
Type: REPORT FORM tranrep1 TO PRINT.

Key words

Edit 2, 4, 5, 6, 12, 13, 17, 12, 14, 27
Report 12, 14, 27

Task 14 Altering a report specification

Objective

To alter the content and layout of an existing report form.

Instructions

The MODIFY REPORT command is used to make changes to a report form. Make two changes to TRANREP1; the first to add an extra column to show the DEPT field, in an otherwise identical report; the second to produce the report in summary form only.

Activity 14.1

Inserting an extra column

1 Open TRANS with index TREFI.
2 Type MODIFY REPORT TRANREP1.
3 Highlight (do not select) COLUMNS from the menu bar.
4 Press the PGDN until you get to column 4 (amount).
5 Press CTRL–N to insert a column, press RETURN TO select, and specify its contents as DEPT, its heading as Dept. (Note what is happening in the status bar below as you do these).
6 Select EXIT from the menu bar and SAVE the report form file.
7 Type REPORT FORM narep1 HEADING "Activity 14, Exercise 1" TO PRINT.

Activity 14.2

Printing summary information only

1 Open TRANS with index TREFI.
2 Type MODIFY REPORT TRANREP1.
3 Highlight GROUPS from the menu bar, and select SUMMARY REPORT ONLY. Set it to YES.
4 EXIT, SAVE, and print the REPORT as above, this time with the extra heading 'Activity 14.2: Summary'.

Activity 14.3

Deleting a column

1 Open TRANS with index TREFI.
2 Type MODIFY REPORT TRANREP1.
3 Highlight GROUPS and select SUMMARY GROUPS ONLY. Set it back to NO. (This has nothing to do with deleting columns, but sets TRANREP1 back to what it was before Activity 14.2).
4 Highlight COLUMNS, and use the PGDN key to select column 4 (DEPT).
5 Press CTRL–U
6 EXIT, SAVE and print the new REPORT with the extra heading: 'Activity 14.3: Departments removed'.

Key words	Modify 6, 12, 16, 17, 18, 21, 27 Report 12, 13, 27

Task 15 Report column contents

Objective

To edit fields going into a report, and to vary the contents of a column at the time of printing.

Instructions

So far, the column contents have simply been unedited fields from the database.

To edit fields to get rid of trailing spaces, or to ensure a specific number of decimal places, the TRIM() OR STR() functions can be used.

There are also instances when the contents of a column will vary. For example, to list all the customers' details, and highlight those whose balances are overdrawn with the words 'Credit Limit Overdrawn' in the right-most column, the IIF command is used.

TRIM() and STR()

To illustrate the use of these two functions, edit the names printed in column 2 and the credit limits in column 3, in the Current Customer Accounts Summary Report. In that report, FIRSTNAME and SURNAME each took up the width of its field in the database, and so appeared widely spaced when printed.

Activity 15.1

Open the NAMADD database, and alter the report form created at the end of Task 12, NAREP2.
Highlight COLUMNS, press PGDN and select column 2.
The use of upper or lower case letters is unimportant. With that proviso, be careful to check your typing as you alter the CONTENTS (put INS on if it is not already – check the command line below) as follows:

TRIM(title)+" "+TRIM(firstname)+" "+TRIM(surname)

Press **PGDN** to highlight column 3 CRLIM
Alter the contents of this to STR(crlim,8,2)
The STR() function: STR(<expression[,<length>][,<decimal>] converts the printed CRLIM to a character string eight characters wide, of which three are used for a decimal point and *two* decimal places. It is useful for specifying a specific field format. Take care to make sure that the overall length can accommodate the maximum value likely to be placed in it, including any minus sign, decimal point, and decimal places.
EXIT, SAVE, and print the NAREP2 report with the extra heading 'Activity 15.1: Edited Names'.
Compare the way in which customer names are now printed against the original version. TRIM has removed all leading or trailing spaces from the three fields to be printed in column 2. The addition of the +" " variables ensured that one space would separate each element.
Note There is no longer a total of credit limits – they are being treated as character, not numeric, for this report, as a result of the STR() function.

Instructions "Immediate IF": IIF()

The Immediate IF function is useful for replacing the contents of a variable with one of a possible two values according to the current situation it finds at the time. To illustrate this, add a column to the TRANREP1 report to print out either "*****" or nothing, according to whether or not the transaction amount is more than 99.99. This can be done as follows:

Activity 15.2

1 Open trans database, and modify TRANREP1 report form to insert column 6.
2 Set its contents to the following:
IIF(amount > 99.99, "*****"," ")
This means IF, in the current database record, the value in AMOUNT is more than 99.99, then in this column print "*****", otherwise leave it blank.
3 EXIT, SAVE, and then print out the new TRANREP1 report, with the extra heading 'Activity 15.2: Highlighting sales over £100'.

Key words

Function 7, 9, 16, 28
Iif
Str
Trim

Task 16 Labels

Objective

To specify the dimensions and contents of a label format for printing standard labels.

Instructions

The labels facility in dBASE is useful for producing name and address labels to go on envelopes or packages, stock labels to go on warehouse packaging, etc.

There are five predefined label sizes from which to choose, or alternatively you can specify your own. One, two or three labels may be printed across. Obviously, the settings you choose must match the actual label stationery to be used.

After working through the creation and use of report formats in tasks 12 to 15, the setting up of label formats will be relatively simple.

Activity 16

To produce name and address labels from the NAMADD database:
Open the database and type: MODIFY LABEL NA
The screen clears to display the menu bar with OPTIONS, CONTENTS and EXIT.
Cursor movement and selection of choices are exactly as in the modify report menu.
Select OPTIONS.
Select the standard label size 2, by pressing RETURN on the highlighted PREDEFINED SIZE.
This will print two labels across, on labels measuring 89mm wide by 24mm high.
Select CONTENTS from across the menu bar and specify how the actual data from the current database is to be printed.
Press RETURN to select Label Contents 1
Type TRIM(Title) +" " +LEFT(firstname,1) +" " +SURNAME into Label Contents 1.
The LEFT function extracts left-most characters from the field or string specified, the number of characters being the second parameter specified within the brackets. In this example we have picked out the firstname initial.
Press RETURN then move cursor down to next contents.
If you are unsure of fieldnames, use the F10 key and highlight the fieldname from those listed, then press RETURN to automatically insert it in the label entry you are specifying.
Pressing RETURN to select, and again to complete, each entry:
Specify LINE1 for Label contents 2
Specify LINE2 for Label contents 3
Specify LINE3 for Label contents 4
Specify POSTCODE for Label contents 5.
Select EXIT from across the menu bar and SAVE the label format file.
This will be written on to the disk with .LBL appended to its name, so the label format file just created will appear as NA.LBL in your directory.
To print out the labels, first load the required stationery – normally continuous self-adhesive labels, but for this purpose use standard paper.
The command to print labels is:
LABEL FORM <label filename> [<scope>] [SAMPLE] [FOR <condition>] [TO PRINT/ TO FILE<filename>]
Make sure the printer is on-line, and then type LABEL FORM na SAMPLE TO PRINT
Print test labels first by including SAMPLE in the command to ensure that the special stationery is properly aligned. The test label will be printed again until you type N in answer to the question 'Do you want more samples?'.
Try also: LABEL FORM NA FOR BAL > CRLIM

Key words	Create 1, 12, 17, 26, 27 File 1, 2, 11, 12, 17, 19, 27 For 3, 4, 5, 10 Function 7, 9, 15, 28 Label Left Modify 6, 12, 17, 18, 21, 27

Task 17

Designing and using an input screen layout

Objective

To create, or modify, a customised screen display to be used when inputting or deleting records on the current database.

Instructions

You have seen how creating your own report format files can greatly improve the presentation of any printouts produced by LIST or DISPLAY. In earlier tasks you were shown how to use EDIT and APPEND to alter, delete, or insert records at the dot prompt. Creating your own screen format files can similarly improve the look and 'user-friendliness' of the screen when updating a database.

CREATE SCREEN is used to specify a new screen format file, with .SCR appended to the filename you give.

MODIFY SCREEN is used to specify a new, or alter an existing, screen format file.

When you save the .SCR file, a second file with .FMT appended to the filename is also created. This second file is in fact a short program, and we will look at its contents in a later task.

You can now specify how the screen should look when you input new, or alter existing, records on the name and address database. The area for 'drawing' your design is called the blackboard and takes up rows 1 to 20 inclusive on the screen. You can alternate between blackboard and menus using the F10 key.

If at any point you make a mistake, select EXIT ABANDON from the menu bar to wipe out the .SCR file you have been working on, and start again. (Once you have had practice in drawing screen layouts you will be able to correct any mistakes without having to go right back to the beginning.)

The aim of this activity is to design a screen display as shown opposite.

Activity 17.1

Defining the screen contents

Open the NAMADD database, and type: CREATE SCREEN NA

A menu bar across the top of the screen will now display the options: SET UP, MODIFY, OPTIONS, and EXIT.

The SET UP menu is already highlighted, and the database has already been selected by opening it at (1) above.

Highlight LOAD FIELDS and press RETURN

A list of fieldnames will appear, from which to select those to appear in the screen layout. In this case, all of them are needed, because the screen will be used whenever you wish to alter an old, or insert a new, customer's details.

Select each by pressing RETURN. As you do so an arrow will appear to the left of each name.

When all have been selected, press the right-arrow key to leave that menu and obtain the Screen Field Definition Blackboard.

This shows fieldnames and, in reverse video, their data input areas alongside, corresponding in size and type to the fields as defined in the database structure.

Start re-positioning these data input areas anywhere on the screen that you want.

Look at the intended screen layout again, then follow the instructions carefully.

```
----------------------------------------------------------------------
0                                                        Screen Ref: NA

1

2                          NAME & ADDRESS FILE UPDATE

3

4

5          CUSTOMER REF: ____        DATE OF OPENING ACCOUNT: __/__/__

6

7 MR/MRS/MS/MISS:____ FIRSTNAME:________________ SURNAME:_______________

8

9          ADDRESS: ____________________

10

11                  ____________________

12

13                  ____________________

14

15        POSTCODE: __________

16

17         CREDIT LIMIT: ____            MONTHLY REPAYMENT: ____.__

18

19         CURRENT BALANCE: _____.__

20
----------------------------------------------------------------------
```

Note The numbers on the left are for reference in the acitivity which follows, and are not part of the screen design.

Instructions

Using the blackboard

Do NOT press RETURN unless specifically told to do so.
Put INSert on and leave on for the rest of the exercise.

Note that the status bar below constantly indicates the page, row, and column that the cursor is in (currently Pg 01 row 00 col 00) and that row and column numbers start

at 00, not 01.
This will be useful in the instructions which follow.
Row and column co-ordinates will be written as: ROW row number/column number (e.g. row 01/00)

Cursor movement can be controlled with the arrow keys, or with CTRL–F (to jump to the beginning of the next word or field), or with the tab key to insert and jump eight spaces at a time. A word can be deleted with CTRL–T, a character with CTRL–G or DEL.

If you delete part of a field's data input area by mistake, move the cursor into the area again and press INS once to increase its size by one character. Repeat if necessary.

Activity 17.2

Rows 00 – 04

The cursor is on the R of REF. Press RETURN four times to insert four blank rows.
Use the arrow and tab keys to move the cursor back to Row 00/62, and type (Screen Ref: NA)
Move the cursor to row 02/26, and type: NAME & ADDRESS FILE UPDATE
Press RETURN

Row 05

Press CTRL–F to move the cursor to REF at row 05/00.
Type (ten spaces) CUSTOMER (one space)
Move the cursor to the other side of REF and insert the colon (:)
Press CTRL–G eight times to delete some spaces between 'REF:' and its data input area.
Move the cursor to row 05/36, and type:
DATE OF OPENING ACCOUNT: (1 space)
Move the cursor to row 13/00 and press CTRL–T to delete 'OPENED'.
The cursor is now inside the OPENED data input area.
To 'drag' this area up to row 5 into its new position, carry out the following three steps (note what happens in the prompt lines below):
Press RETURN once
Move the cursor to row 05/61
Press RETURN again.
OPENED will have moved from row 13 to row 5.
Before you continue with the design, store what you have done so far:
Press F10 to get back to the menus
Select EXIT and SAVE to save the NA.SCR file onto disk and get back to the dot prompt.
The design is continued on the following pages.
If you are interrupted at any point while still working on a screen design, save it as here and continue later.
To re-start, first open the NAMADD database, and set INS on.
Type MODIFY SCREEN NA
and press F10 to get back to the Blackboard.

Rows 06 – 07

Move the cursor to row 06/00, and press RETURN Type:
(3 spaces) MR/MRS/MISS/MS: (6 spaces)
Move the cursor to row 07/33, insert a colon after FIRSTNAME, then press CTRL–G twice.
Move cursor to col 52 and type SURNAME: (1 space)
Press CTRL–F, then CTRL–T to delete 'Surname' from row 8.
The cursor is inside the SURNAME data entry area. Drag it up to line 7 by pressing RETURN once, move cursor to row 07/61, press RETURN once.
Move the cursor to row 09/00 and press CTRL–T to delete 'Title'. The cursor is inside the TITLE data entry area. Drag it up to row 07/19.

Row 09

Move the cursor to row 09/00. Press CTRL–Y to delete the blank line.
Press CTRL–T once to delete 'LINE1', then type:
(ten spaces) ADDRESS: (one space)
(LINE1 data entry area is now at row 09/19)

Rows 10 – 15

Move the cursor to row 10/00. Press RETURN once.
Press CTRL–T to delete 'LINE2'. Insert 19 spaces.
Move the cursor to row 12/00. Press RETURN once.
Press CTRL–T to delete 'LINE3'. Insert 19 spaces.
Move the cursor to row 14/00. Press RETURN once.
Insert nine spaces in front of 'POSTCODE' and a colon (:) after it. Delete three spaces after it, to line up the data entry area with the rest of the address.

Rows 16 – 19

Move cursor to Row 17/00. Delete 'CRLIM', and type:
(9 spaces) CREDIT LIMIT: (1 space)
At row 17 col 42 type MONTHLY REPAYMENT: (1 space)
At row 18/00 delete 'REPAY'. This leaves the cursor in the REPAY data input area. Drag this up to row 17 col 61.
At row 19/00 delete 'BAL'. Type (9 spaces) CURRENT BALANCE: (1 space)
Your screen design is now complete.
Press the F10 key to get back the menus.
Select EXIT SAVE to store the design on disk, and return to the dot prompt.
To try it out, type SET FORMAT TO NA
APPEND
The SET FORMAT command tells dBASE which screen format to use.
The screen will clear, and then display your own data input screen (NA.SCR) instead of the customary one. The cursor is in the first field (REF) entry area ready to accept your record details. Create a record with your own personal details, leaving balance blank.
A second screen will automatically appear after completing the details for this 'customer'.
To finish and save the appended record, press RETURN while the cursor is in REF.
The screen can be cleared by typing CLEAR at the dot prompt.

Key words	
Key words	**Create 1, 12, 16, 26, 27** **Edit 2, 4, 5, 6, 12, 13** **File 1, 2, 11, 12, 16, 19, 27** **Menu bar 12, 27** **Modify 6, 12, 16, 18, 21, 27** **Set format 19** **Screen 19**

Task 18

An introduction to programming in dBASE III +

Objective

To learn what a dBASE Program is and how to write one.

Instructions

A dBASE III Plus program, like a program written in any other computer language, is a list of instructions or commands, which the computer will perform in sequence, automatically, in order to carry out a particular task. You have already been using some of the dBASE language throughout this Training Guide, whenever you have given instructions at the dot prompt.

A series of commands becomes a program when you store them altogether in a single file and the name of this file becomes the name of your program. Whenever you need to issue all those commands again, rather than type them all out again, a single instruction will allow you to run the program. Programs can be linked together to form a complete system carrying out many tasks. A main program, started with a single command by the user, can display the options available, and automatically call and run the corresponding program modules, according to what is selected.

Having used some of the dBASE III Plus language, to create and manipulate simple databases, you can now make your database management system faster, easier and safer for you and others, to use.

For writing or editing a dBASE III program, there is a built-in word processor, called at the dot prompt by typing MODIFY COMMAND <program filename>.

The suffix .PRG is automatically put onto the end of the program filename given, which enables you to distinguish program files from any others in your directory.

CTRL–W quits the word processor and saves the edited program.
ESC quits the word processor without saving the edited program.

We already have two databases, NAMADD and TRANS. These will be used in our programs, the first few of which will introduce you to a number of new commands specifically used and/or useful in programs.

Activity 18.1

Program 1: PROGNA1

At the dot prompt, type MODIFY COMMAND PROGNA1
The screen clears to display the word processor menu above the blank editing area.
Use the menu as your guide in the case of any typing errors.
Enter the program as shown in the following screen display, taking care to check your typing. *Note* The most common errors are mis-spelt commands, missing spaces (between command and/or parameters), and incomplete commands.
When you have finished, press CTRL–END.

```
****    ProgNA1
****    Written in: ACTIVITY 18.1
****    To alter details in an existing record in NAMADD database

SET DATE BRITISH
USE NAMADD
SET FORMAT TO NA
CLEAR
?
?
?
?
? "                              NAME and ADDRESS File"
?
? "                          Amendment to Customer details"
?
?
ACCEPT "                         Enter the Customer's Reference: " TO mvref
?
? "                Press Ctrl-End after you have made your alterations"
?
WAIT "               Press any key to obtain the data entry screen   "
EDIT FOR REF = UPPER(mvref)
CLEAR
RETURN
**** End of ProgNA1 ****
```

In this program, you have used the following new commands:

? <expression list>
issues a carriage return before displaying the expression list.
On its own, ? outputs one blank line

Wait <prompt>
causes the program to temporarily stop until a key is entered.
'PRESS ANY KEY TO CONTINUE..' is displayed if no prompt is specified.
Clear clears the screen
Return ends the program and returns control to the dot prompt
**** Lines beginning with an asterisk are comment lines, useful for putting explanatory remarks into a program listing.

Instructions

Testing the program
It is always essential to test your program to check that it does what it is intended to do. If you have not done any programming before, bear in mind that when the computer is instructed to run a program, it will blindly carry out the instructions, one after the other in sequence starting with the first. It will attempt to do this even if you have unwittingly mis-typed any, or put them in the wrong sequence, or told it to do something illogical. The command to start a program is DO <program name>

Activity 18.2

Print out REF, OPENED and BAL from the whole NAMADD file before you start. This will help later when checking whether your program works or not.

Make sure that all files are closed and the memory is cleared, prior to a test run, by typing CLEAR ALL.

To run the program, type DO PROGNA1 and alter the record for customer S001, setting date of opening to 1 December, and balance to 2.75. Press RETURN after giving the customer reference, and follow the instructions on screen. When the custom screen is displayed move from field to field using the RETURN key. As soon as you have entered 2.75 the program will automatically end, and return you to the dot prompt.

If the program does not work as expected, check your program listing and correct any mistakes you find in it. This is done by using the same MODIFY COMMAND as in (1) above, except that the program listing will now appear on screen when you call the word processor.

Run PROGNA1 again to alter the following balances:

REF	BALANCE	REF	BALANCE
c001	151.50	m001	118.09

With this test data, the program should convert your lower case letters (c, m) to capitals automatically. Does it?

Try running it again to see what happens when you put in a REF of XYZZ. It should allow you to enter it, but will then just end without doing, or reporting, anything.

Print out REF, OPENED and BAL from the whole file again, to see and check the effect of your tests. Have the balance figures been altered to the required values on the required records?

Finally, to obtain a hard copy of your program listing, do not use LIST or DISPLAY. Instead use the TYPE command. Type TYPE progna1.prg TO PRINT

Activity 18.3

Write a similar program, entitled PROGNA2, which APPENDS new customer records to the NAMADD database.

Test your program with test data of your own until you are satisfied that it works as intended.

Print out the program listing.

A possible solution is found at the end of this Task.

Activity 18.4

PROGNA3

Write a program which DELETES a customer's record from the NAMADD database. You could use either EDIT with CTRL–U, or DELETE FOR . . . , to mark the record for the deletion. Do not include PACK at this stage.

Test your program, by deleting the records you have inserted in Activity 18.2. When you print out the file, the records will have an asterisk alongside the REF to indicate their being marked for deletion. Once satisfied that this works correctly, PACK the file to delete the records.

Print out the program records.

A possible solution is shown at the end of this Task.

Key words

?
Clear 2
Clear all 20
Cmonth 9
Do 20, 23, 24
List 3, 7, 9, 25
Modify Command 18–28
Pack 5
Program 19, 20, 21, 23
Return
Type 19
Wait

```
*****   ProgNA2
*****   Written in: ACTIVITY 18.3:
*****   To insert a record in NAMADD database

SET DATE BRITISH
USE NAMADD
SET FORMAT TO NA
CLEAR
?
?
?
?
? "                          NAME and ADDRESS File"
?
? "                     INSERTING NEW CUSTOMERS' DETAILS"
?
?
? "             To finish, press RETURN when presented with"
? "                        fresh input screen"
?
WAIT "            Press any key to get the data entry screen now"
APPEND
CLEAR
RETURN
**** End of ProgNA2 ****
```

```
****  ProgNA3
****  ACTIVITY 18.4
****  To delete a Customer from NAMADD ****

SET DATE BRITISH
USE NAMADD
CLEAR
? "Date: ",DATE()
?
?
?
? "                          NAME and ADDRESS File"
?
? "                        Delete a Customer's Record"
?
?
ACCEPT "            Enter the Customer's Reference : " TO MVREF
?
DELETE FOR REF = UPPER(MVREF)
CLEAR
RETURN
****  End of ProdNA3  ****
```

Task 19 Programming: user-friendly screen dialogue

Objective

To use an alternative and better method of displaying prompts, accepting data and checking what is typed.

Instructions

In PROGNA1, the ? Display and ACCEPT commands were used for displaying instructions and receiving data. You had to insert spaces in character strings, and the program was unnecessarily long.

Instead you can use the following:

@ is used to specify the row and column numbers at which to start displaying information. It is usually accompanied with SAY and/or GET. Without any other parameters, @ will delete the row starting at the given column.

@ . . **Say** displays information that you do not want to change.

@ . . **Get** displays and allows to be altered a field or memory variable.

@ . . **Clear** erases the screen below and to the right of the coordinates.

Activity 19.1	Program 4: PROGTR1 Type MODIFY COMMAND PRO6TR1 Enter the program as shown in the listing

Instructions

Range can be used to specify minimum and maximum values to be accepted by GET when used for numeric or date input. It is a useful aid to checking input. If you press RETURN without any data in answer to GET, no range check will be carried.

Picture can be used to format the SAY and GET data variables, and can carry out further checks on what is entered in answer to GET. It comprises a function and/or a template, both within the same pair of quotes characters, and separated from each other by a space. The function always has the @ character preceding it within the quotes. See the three picture clauses in the program and the explanatory notes below.

Read is used to activate full-screen editing of GET fields. What this means is that the program will stop and wait for your entries at the keyboard.

Set talk off prevents display and response of command lines on screen in the middle of a program.

To illustrate the use of @ . . . SAY/GET, enter PROGTR1. The program opens TRANS database and inserts one record containing the details of a customer's purchase.

Note Set talk off prevents (in this instance) the message '1 record(s) inserted' from spoiling the display.

Append blank inserts a blank record at the end of the file, which is then edited by the succeeding GET/READs.

Picture: "@!" is a FUNCTION which converts any letters input to upper case automatically. This ensures that all customer REFerences on file follow this rule. It is separated within the picture clause from the TEMPLATE:

"A999" 'A' signifies that only a letter can be entered in this position

'9' signifies that only a digit can be entered in this position.

Picture: "#" allows only digits, blanks, or a sign. The dot signifies the decimal position.

Range purchases paid on account must be for at least one pound up to a maximum of two thousand pounds.

Replace there is no need to ask the user to input the record type; this will put it in the record automatically.

Activity 19.2 Program 4: PROGTR1

Run PROGTR1 with the following data:
Customer M001 purchase in ladies' Fashion (LF) department amounting to 24.75 on 5/12/88.
Check that this has been put on file correctly by displaying the record on-screen.
Whenever you write or change a program, always run it to test that it works, and check the contents of the record(s) affected. If it has not worked correctly, check your program and make any alterations necessary, then test it again.

```
****     ProgTR2
****     Written by <your own name>
****     ACTIVITY 19.3
****     To input a PAYMENT record onto TRANS database

SET TALK OFF
CLEAR
USE TRANS
APPEND BLANK
SET DATE BRITISH
@00,70 SAY "ProgTR2"
@6,30 SAY  "BUDGET ACCOUNT SYSTEM"
@7,30 SAY  "---------------------"
@9,21 SAY  "PLEASE ENTER CUSTOMER PAYMENT DETAILS"
@12,15 SAY "Customer Ref: " GET ref    PICTURE "@! A999"
@12,45 SAY "Date: "         GET tdate
@15,15 SAY "      Amount: " GET amount PICTURE "###9.99" RANGE 1,2000
READ
REPLACE rec WITH "PAY"
REPLACE amount WITH amount*-1
CLEAR
RETURN
****  End of ProgTR2  ****
```

Activity 19.3 Program 5 : PROGTR2

Write a program PROGTR2 that will allow the user to process a payment received from a customer, storing the details in a record on the TRANS database.
The REC field should be set to 'PAY' by the program.
The AMOUNT entered by the user must be multiplied by –1 so that it is held on record as a negative value.
Test your program with the following data:
Customer S001 Payment of 25.00 on 5/12/88.

```
****     ProgTR1
****     Written by <your own name>
****     ACTIVITY 19.1
****     To input a PURCHASE record onto TRANS database

SET TALK OFF
CLEAR
USE TRANS
APPEND BLANK
SET DATE BRITISH
@00,70 SAY "ProgTR1"
@6,30 SAY  "BUDGET ACCOUNT SYSTEM"
@7,30 SAY  "---------------------"
@9,30 SAY "PLEASE ENTER PURCHASE DETAILS"
@12,15 SAY "Customer Ref: " GET ref     PICTURE "@! A999"
@12,45 SAY "Date: "         GET tdate
@15;15 SAY "       Amount: " GET amount PICTURE "###9.99" RANGE 1,2000
@15,45 SAY "Dept: "         GET dept PICTURE "@!"
READ
REPLACE rec WITH "PUR"
CLEAR
RETURN
****  End of ProgTR1  ****
```

Activity 19.4 Program 6 : PROGTR3

Write a program PROGTR3 which will allow the user to process a return, storing the details in a record on the TRANS database.
The REC field should be set to 'RET', and AMOUNT written as a negative amount.
Test your program with the following data:
Customer M001 returned goods to Ladies' Fashion (LF) department amounting in value to 24.75 on 7/12/88.
There should now be twenty-seven records on the TRANS database.
A possible solution is shown on the following program listing.

```
****     ProgTR3
****     Written by <your own name>
****     ACTIVITY 19.4
****     To input a RETURNS record onto TRANS database

SET TALK OFF
CLEAR
USE TRANS
APPEND BLANK
SET DATE BRITISH
@00,70 SAY "ProgTR3"
@6,30 SAY  "BUDGET ACCOUNT SYSTEM"
@7,30 SAY  "---------------------"
@9,21 SAY  "PLEASE ENTER A CUSTOMER'S RETURN DETAILS"
@12,15 SAY "Customer Ref: " GET ref     PICTURE "@! A999"
@12,45 SAY "Date: "         GET tdate
@15,15 SAY "      Amount: " GET amount  PICTURE "###9.99" RANGE 1,2000
@15,45 SAY "Dept: "         GET dept    PICTURE "@!"
READ
REPLACE rec WITH "RET"
REPLACE amount WITH amount*-1
CLEAR
RETURN
****   End of ProgTR3   ****
```

Activity 19.5 .FMT FILES

When you created/modified the screen to take your input for the NAMADD database, dBASE stored two files on disc: a .SCR file and a .FMT file. The latter is the file brought into action when you SET FORMAT TO. Now look at the .FMT files – you will see that they are command files containing a series of @SAY/GET.
Use the TYPE command to print out the NA format file:
Type : TYPE NA.FMT TO PRINT

Key words

Task 20 Programming: linking two or more programs

Objective

To link two or more programs together, and to automate the decision between two courses of action.

Instructions

The feature which distinguishes a computer from any other electronic data processing aid is its ability to automatically carry out any one of a number of alternate activities according to the circumstances at the time.

One command which makes it examine the circumstances is the IF command. The command used to call and run another program is the DO command, which you have been using already at the dot prompt.

These are illustrated in the seventh program, PROGTR0, which does the following:

a. Displays a short menu of options to the user.

b. Checks the data entered, and calls:

PROGTR1 to insert a purchase record if option 1 is selected, or PROGTR2 to insert a payment record if option 2 is selected.

Activity 20.1

Program 7: PROGTR0

Enter and save PROGTR0 as shown in the program listing that follows.

Note IF <condition> and ELSE are each specified on one line, the dependent actions indented on the following lines, and the whole IF statement brought to an end with the ENDIF.

Indenting the dependent actions is good practice: it makes your programs easier to read, and helps when checking that you have not omitted the required ENDIF.

Store is used to create the memory variable OPT, which, because a number was stored into it, becomes a numeric variable. An alternative way of writing this instruction is in the format:

<memory variable> = <expression>, e.g. OPT = 0

Clear all closes any open database and releases any memory variables used. It is good practice to do this at the start/end of your main program.

"@Z #" This PICTURE clause contains the function Z to show a zero value as blank, and a template of # to indicate only digits, blanks or sign can be entered in the variable OPT.

Range 1, 2 ensures that only the numbers 1 or 2 will be accepted, and so the following IF clause can safely assume this to be the case.

Run the program twice using the following data:

Customer	Type	Date	Amount	Department
T002	Payment	05/12/88	30.00	
S002	Purchase	03/12/88	18.99	CHI

Check the results by displaying these two records. If any mistakes are made, check the program and make any alterations necessary.

```
****     ProgTR0
****     Written by <your own name>
****     ACTIVITY 20.1
****     To choose and process Payment or Purchase

SET TALK OFF
CLEAR ALL
CLEAR
SET DATE BRITISH
@00,70 SAY "ProgTR0"
@6,30 SAY  "BUDGET ACCOUNT SYSTEM"
@7,30 SAY  "---------------------"
@10,20 SAY "1   Process PURCHASE"
@12,20 SAY "2   Process PAYMENT"
STORE 0 TO opt
@16,12 SAY "Please make your selection :"
@16,41 GET opt PICTURE "@Z #" RANGE 1,2
READ
CLEAR
IF opt = 1
   DO progTR1
ELSE
   DO progTR2
ENDIF
RETURN
****  End of ProgTR0  ****
```

Activity 20.2

Program 8: PROGNA0
Write a program, PROGNA0, which displays the two options:
(1) to alter a customer's details;
(2) to insert a new customer's details;
accepts the user's choice and updates the NAMADD database accordingly, using the existing programs PROGNA1 and PROGNA2.

Test your program thoroughly altering customer S002's credit limit to 600, and inserting a record for Ms Grace Roberts, reference R001, whose address and other details you may supply yourself.
A possible solution is shown in the following program listing.

```
****     ProgNA0
****     Written by <your own name>
****     ACTIVITY 20.2
****     To choose & process: AMEND an existing Customer record
****                          or INSERT  a new customer's details.

SET TALK OFF
CLEAR ALL
CLEAR
SET DATE BRITISH
@00,70 SAY "ProgNA0"
@6,30 SAY  "BUDGET ACCOUNT SYSTEM"
@7,30 SAY  "---------------------"
@10,20 SAY "1   AMEND an existing Customer record"
@12,20 SAY "2   INSERT a new Customer's record"
STORE 0 TO opt
@16,12 SAY "Please make your selection :"
@16,41 GET opt PICTURE "@Z #" RANGE 1,2
READ
CLEAR
IF opt = 1
   DO progna1
ELSE
   DO progna2
ENDIF
RETURN
****  End of Progna0  ****
```

Key words

Task 21 Programming: mutiple choices

Objective

To write a program which deals with a multiple of possible options, allowing the user to choose which at run time.

Instructions

In the last exercise, we wrote programs to deal with just two alternative courses of action. Your system will probably offer the user several options. You could use a multiple IF statement, but far simpler would be a command to help in dealing with multiple choice – DO CASE. This is illustrated in the new version of program PROGTR0 below, which allows the user to choose to input purchase, payment, or return – and detects any mis-typing.

Activity 21.1

Program 9: Amended PROGTR0

Edit the original program by deleting commands no longer in the new version (CTRL–Y to delete a row), and inserting new commands (CTRL–N, to create a blank line in which to type), so that the program now reads as on the program listing that follows.

Note 1 indenting the dependent cases within the DO CASE improves readability and helps check that the required ENDCASE statement has not been omitted.
Note 2 The memory variable OPT has been made a character type for a little more flexibility.
Do case can be interpreted as 'Do whichever is the case from the following: If it is the case that OPT contains the value 1 do ProgTR1, and so on'. Each CASE consists of a condition with its dependent action(s) on the following line(s).

Otherwise traps any incorrect input, and illustrates a cardinal rule in programming: never assume that the data which the user is supposed to enter is what they will enter!

Endcase must terminate the complete statement when all cases have been dealt with.

Test (and if necessary amend) the new version of the program until you are sure that it works correctly for:
(a) purchases (b) payments (c) returns (d) invalid input
To be certain that your program works correctly, print out and check the contents of TRANS both before and after you run it. When you have completed testing, print out your program for reference.

```
****     PROGTRO
****     Written by <your own name>
****     ACTIVITY 21.1
****     To choose & process: Payment or Purchase or Return-of-goods

SET TALK OFF
CLEAR ALL
CLEAR
SET DATE BRITISH
@00,70 SAY "ProgTRO"
@6,30 SAY  "BUDGET ACCOUNT SYSTEM"
@7,30 SAY  "---------------------"
@10,30 SAY "1   Process PURCHASE"
@12,30 SAY "2   Process PAYMENT"
@14,30 SAY "3   Process RETURN"
STORE " " TO opt
@16,12 SAY "Please make your selection :" GET opt PICTURE "@Z #"
READ
CLEAR
DO CASE
   CASE opt = "1"
        DO progTR1
   CASE opt = "2"
        DO progTR2
   CASE opt = "3"
        DO progTR3
   OTHERWISE
        @16,12 CLEAR
        @16,12 SAY "INCORRECT OPTION NUMBER, PLEASE START AGAIN"
ENDCASE
RETURN
****  End of ProgTRO /Program 9 ****
```

Activity 21.2 Program 10: Amended version of PROGNA0

Alter the program PROGNA0 so that the user can select to either insert, amend or delete a customer's account details on the NAMADD database, or be informed of any incorrect input. Close the database and clear the memory at the end of the program.

Test the program thoroughly for all possible types of input, and obtain a printed program listing on completion.

A possible solution is shown in the following program listing.

```
****     ProgNAO
****     Amended by <your own name>
****     ACTIVITY 21.2
****     To choose & process: AMEND an existing Customer record
****                          or INSERT  a new customer's details.

SET TALK OFF
CLEAR ALL
CLEAR
SET DATE BRITISH
@00,70 SAY "ProgNAO"
@6,30 SAY  "BUDGET ACCOUNT SYSTEM"
@7,30 SAY  "---------------------"
@10,20 SAY "1   AMEND an existing Customer record"
@12,20 SAY "2   INSERT a new Customer's record"
@14,20 SAY "3   DELETE a Customer's record"
STORE " " TO opt
@16,12 SAY "Please make your selection :" GET opt PICTURE "@Z #"
READ
CLEAR
DO CASE
   CASE opt = "1"
        DO progna1
   CASE opt = "2"
        DO progna2
   CASE opt = "3"
        DO progna3
   OTHERWISE
        CLEAR
        @16,12 SAY "INCORRECT OPTION NUMBER - PLEASE START AGAIN
ENDCASE
RETURN
****  End of PrognaO  / Program 10   ****
```

Key words

Task 22

Programming: automatic repetition

Objective

To make the program automatically repeat its procedures as often as required.

Instructions

The program still only processes one record at a time. You can now make it fully automatic.

The DO WHILE command causes all the statements between it and its matching ENDDO to be repeated for as long as a specified condition remains true. An intervening EXIT allows you to jump out of the loop at that point, and a LOOP allows you to branch back to the beginning of the DO at that point.

The format is as follows, and must always end with ENDDO :

DO WHILE <condition>
    <commands>
    [EXIT]
    <commands>
    [LOOP]
    <commands>
ENDDO

Activity 22.1

Program 11: Amended version of PROGTRO

Program PROGTRO can be made to automatically repeat the display and processing of different options, until the user indicates that he has finished. To do this, again alter the main program PROGTRO, and introduce a further option (9), by which the user can indicate the end of their processing (and thereby terminate the DO loop).

Alter the program PROGTRO so that it reads as in the program listing that follows.

&& allows you to include comments in the program listing. They have been used here to indicate which lines have been changed in this version (ignoring those which were only altered to indent them for readability.).

Loop In the last versions of PROGTRO and PROGNA0 (programs 9 and 10), if an option of, say, 5 was entered, the error would simply be reported (in the OTHERWISE clause) and the program would stop (it would just drop through the ENDCASE). Here, the OTHERWISE clause (followed if the user does not enter 1,2,3, or 9) includes LOOP which will enable the user to repeat his input, by causing the program to continue from the beginning of the DO WHILE statement.

Exit causes the program to continue from the statement immediately after the ENDDO.

Test your program thoroughly for all possible options, correct and incorrect. If any program alterations are necessary, always re-test it. When satisfied, obtain a printed program listing.

```
****   PROGTRO
****   Amended <date>
****   ACTIVITY 22.1
****   To repeatedly process Payments Purchases and Returns until
****                                                  the user selects option 9

CLEAR ALL
SET TALK OFF
SET DATE BRITISH
STORE 0 TO opt
USE TRANS
DO WHILE .not. opt = 9
   CLEAR
   @0,70 SAY  "PROGTRO"
   @6,30 SAY  "BUDGET ACCOUNT SYSTEM"
   @7,30 SAY  "---------------------"
   @10,30 SAY "1   Process PURCHASE"
   @12,30 SAY "2   Process PAYMENT "
   @14,30 SAY "3   Process RETURN"
   @16,30 SAY "9   Exit from program"
   STORE 0 TO opt
   @18,12 SAY "Please make your selection :"
   @18,41 GET opt PICTURE "@Z #" RANGE 1,9
   READ
   CLEAR
   DO CASE
      CASE opt = 1
        DO progTR1
      CASE opt = 2
        DO progTR2
      CASE opt = 3
        DO progTR3
      CASE opt = 9         && Prog11
        EXIT               && Prog11
   OTHERWISE
      @17,12 CLEAR
      @19,12 SAY "INCORRECT OPTION NUMBER, PLEASE TRY AGAIN"
      WAIT
      LOOP                   && Prog11
   ENDCASE
ENDDO
RETURN
****   End of ProgTRO / Program 11 ****
```

Activity 22.2 Program 12: Amended version of PROGNA0

Alter program PROGNA0 so that it will repeat the display and processing of options until an option value of 9 is entered by the user. Test the program thoroughly and then obtain a program listing.
A possible solution is shown in the following program listing.

```
****    ProgNAO
****    Amended by <your own name>
****    ACTIVITY 22.2
****    To repeatedly process: AMEND INSERT or DELETE customer
****                            records

SET TALK OFF
CLEAR ALL
SET DATE BRITISH
STORE 0 TO opt
USE NAMADD
DO WHILE .NOT. opt = 9
   CLEAR
   @00,70 SAY "ProgNAO"
   @6,30 SAY  "BUDGET ACCOUNT SYSTEM"
   @7,30 SAY  "---------------------"
   @10,20 SAY "1   AMEND an existing Customer record"
   @12,20 SAY "2   INSERT a new Customer's record"
   @14,20 SAY "3   DELETE a Customer's record"
   @16,20 SAY "9   EXIT from system"
   STORE 0 TO opt
   @18,12 SAY "Please make your selection :"
   @18,41 GET opt PICTURE "@Z #"
   READ
   DO CASE
      CASE opt = 1
           DO progna1
      CASE opt = 2
           DO progna2
      CASE opt = 3
           DO progna3
      CASE opt = 9
           EXIT
      OTHERWISE
           @17,12 CLEAR
           @19,12 SAY "INCORRECT OPTION NUMBER - PLEASE TRY AGAIN
           WAIT
           LOOP
   ENDCASE
   USE
ENDDO
RETURN
****  End of Progna0  / Program 12  ****
```

Key words	&&
	Do while/End do
	Exit
	Loop

Task 23

Passing parameters between programs

Objective

To write a single control program to accept whatever options are input and pass them onto the programs using them.

Instructions

Your programs so far have been split between those which update the NAMADD database, and those which update TRANS. In the finished system you would want a single program to call up any routine, whatever the files used or the processing carried out.

In the following activity you will write a new program which offers a complete menu of all processing in the budget account system. You will also amend the existing TR programs quite drastically, such that programs TR2 and 3 become redundant, and the NA programs only slightly.

The new program and new versions of others will illustrate how data can be passed from one program to another to be used by it.

The new program will be called BAS.prg (for 'Budget Account System'), and will also call two further new programs (to be developed in the final tasks). These are:

PROGREPO to allow the user to select and print a number of reports; and

PROGMTHO to clear down the TRANS file at month end and update the customer balances.

Activity 23.1

Program 13: BAS

Enter BAS.PRG as shown in the following program listing. This accepts the user's option number, evaluates it and calls the required program to do the associated processing. Two of these programs, PROGTRO and PROGNAO, will also need to examine the option number so that they in turn can call appropriate further programs. BAS.PRG passes the option number, input by the user, to them by including the WITH <parameter> in the DO command.

PROGTRO and PROGNAO will in turn 'receive' it by means of the PARAMETERS statement right at their start (comment lines may precede). The parameters linking two programs must always correspond in number sequence and type.

```
****  BAS.prg
****  ACTIVITY 23.1
*    This is the main program in the BUDGET ACCOUNT SYSTEM
*
CLEAR ALL
SET DATE BRITISH
SET ECHO OFF
SET TALK OFF
STORE " " TO opt
DO WHILE opt < "9"
   CLEAR
   STORE " " TO opt
   @00,72 SAY "BAS.prg"
   @02,30 SAY "BUDGET ACCOUNT SYSTEM"
   @03,30 SAY "---------------------"
   @05,27 SAY "Select one of the following:"
   @07,10 SAY "1  Process PURCHASES"
   @07,35 SAY "5  Amend Customer details"
   @09,10 SAY "2  Process PAYMENTS"
   @09,35 SAY "6  Enter NEW customer details"
   @11,10 SAY "3  Process Returns"
   @11,35 SAY "7  Delete Customer details"
   @13,10 SAY "4  REPORTS"
   @13,35 SAY "8  Month-end & Housekeeping Routines"
   @15,15 SAY "Any other key will terminate the system"
   @17,10 SAY "ENTER SELECTED NUMBER HERE: " GET opt
   READ
   CLEAR
   DO CASE
      CASE opt < "4"
           DO progtr0 WITH opt
      CASE opt = "4"
           DO progrep0
      CASE opt > "4" .AND. opt < "8"
           DO progna0 with opt
      CASE opt = "8"
           DO progmth0
      OTHERWISE
           EXIT
   ENDCASE
ENDDO
CLEAR ALL
* End of BAS.PRG / Program 13 *
```

Activity 23.2 Programs 14 and 15: PROGTR0 and PROGTR1 Amendments

Alter these as shown on the program listings. The changes made mean that these two programs now do the work of all four earlier TR programs.

```
****   PROGTRO
****   Amended <date>
****   ACTIVITY 23.2
****   To process Payments Purchases and Returns according to
****      what the user has selected in BAS.PRG

PARAMETERS opt
USE TRANS
CLEAR
mrec = "   "
message = "         "
DO CASE
      CASE opt = "1"
           mrec = "PUR"
           message = "PURCHASE"
      CASE opt = "2"
           mrec = "PAY"
           message = "PAYMENT"
      CASE opt = "3"
           mrec = "RET"
           message = "RETURNS"
   OTHERWISE
      @17,12 CLEAR
      @18,12 SAY "INCORRECT OPTION NUMBER, PLEASE TRY AGAIN"
      WAIT
      RETURN
ENDCASE
DO PROGTR1 WITH mrec,message
CLEAR
RETURN
****   End of ProgTRO /Program 14 ****
```

```
****    ProgTR1
****    Written by <your own name>
****    ACTIVITY 23.2

PARAMETERS mrec,message
APPEND BLANK
@00,70 SAY "ProgTR1"
@6,30 SAY  "BUDGET ACCOUNT SYSTEM"
@7,30 SAY  "---------------------"
@9,30 SAY "PLEASE ENTER "+message+" DETAILS"
@12,15 SAY "Customer Ref: " GET ref     PICTURE "@! A999"
@12,45 SAY "Date: "         GET tdate
@15,15 SAY "     Amount: " GET amount PICTURE "###9.99" RANGE 1,2000
IF .NOT. mrec = "PAY"
    @15,45 SAY "Dept: "         GET dept PICTURE "@!"
ENDIF
REPLACE rec WITH mrec
READ
IF .NOT. mrec = "PUR"
   REPLACE amount WITH amount*-1
ENDIF
RETURN
****   End of ProgTR1 / Program 15 ****
```

Activity 23.3 Programs PROGNA0, 1, 2, and 3
Alter program PROGNA0 so that it receives the parameter OPT.
Alter programs PROGNA1, 2, and 3 to remove the commands which open the file, set date, and clear the screen. These are all done once in PROGNA0 or BAS prior to calling these three programs, and so are no longer needed at this level.
You should have the following screen displays:

```
****     ProgNA0
****     Amended by <your own name>
****     ACTIVITY 23.3
****     To process: AMEND INSERT or DELETE according to
****                 what the user has selected in BAS.prg

PARAMETERS opt
USE NAMADD
CLEAR
DO CASE
      CASE opt = "5"
           DO progna1
      CASE opt = "6"
           DO progna2
      CASE opt = "7"
           DO progna3
      OTHERWISE
           CLEAR
           @18,12 SAY "INCORRECT OPTION NUMBER - PLEASE TRY AGAIN"
           WAIT
ENDCASE
USE
RETURN
****  End of Progna0  / Program 16  ****
```

```
****    ProgNA1
****    ACTIVITY 23.3
****    To alter details in an existing record in NAMADD database

SET FORMAT TO NA
?
?
?
?
? "                         NAME and ADDRESS File"
?
? "                     Amendment to Customer details"
?
?
ACCEPT "                 Enter the Customer's Reference: " TO mvref
?
? "             Press Ctrl-End after you have made your alterations"
?
WAIT "              Press any key to obtain the data entry screen  "
EDIT FOR REF = UPPER(mvref)
RETURN
**** End of ProgNA1 /Program 17 ****
```

```
*****    ProgNA2
*****    ACTIVITY 23.3
*****    To insert a record in NAMADD database

SET FORMAT TO NA
?
?
?
?
? "                         NAME and ADDRESS File"
?
? "                   INSERTING NEW CUSTOMERS' DETAILS"
?
?
? "            Press RETURN after you have made your alterations"
? "                     to return to the dot prompt"
?
WAIT "             Press any key to get the data entry screen now"
APPEND
RETURN
**** End of ProgNA2 / Program 18 ****
```

```
****   ProgNA3
****   ACTIVITY 23.3
****   To delete a Customer from NAMADD ****

? "Date: ",DATE()
?
?
?
? "                                  NAME and ADDRESS File"
?
? "                               Delete a Customer's Record"
?
?
ACCEPT "               Enter the Customer's Reference : " TO MVREF
?
DELETE FOR REF = UPPER(MVREF)
RETURN
****   End of ProgNA3 / Program 19 ****
```

Activity 23.4 Test the system

Because of all the changes made, every single program must be tested again. Using test data of your own making, run BAS.prg, selecting options 1 to 3, 5 to 6, and 9(exit).
If all the changes have been made correctly, your system will repeatedly present you with the main budget account system menu, processing the options you select, and ending when you enter option 9

The budget account system can now be shown diagrammatically as follows:

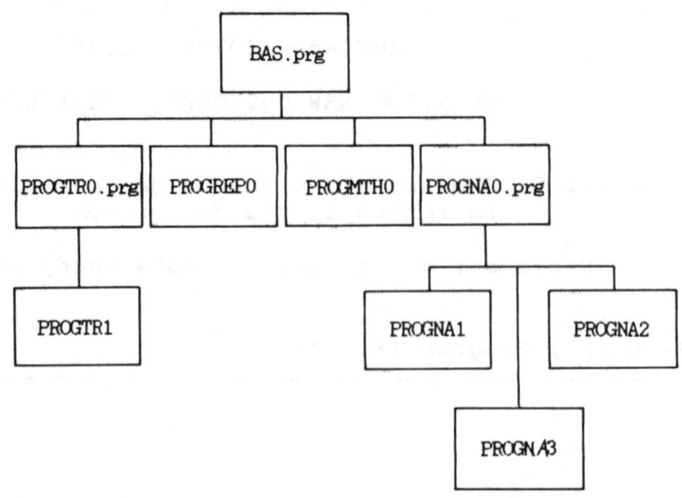

Key words **Do 18, 20, 24**
Do With
Parameter 3
Program 18, 19, 20, 21

Task 24 Programming consolidation exercise: reports program

Objective

To write a program which displays the reports options to the user and prints out whichever are selected.

Instructions

Because there will be several reports to choose from, this program should first display a further menu giving the available options. The suggested format is shown below.

Activity 24.1

Write program 20, entitled PROGREP0, which is the command file called by the main program when the user selects option 4 REPORTS.

Budget account system

Select one of the following:
1 Name and address print
2 Transactions listing
3 Address labels
4 Departmental summary
5 Customers' credit status report
6 Customer statements
9 Return to main menu

ENTER OPTION NUMBER HERE:

Check that the printer is online

The processing should then deal with the user's choice as follows:
Option 1 opens NAMADD with REFI index, and uses report form NAREP1.
Option 2 opens TRANS with TREFI index, and uses report form TRANREP1.
Option 3 opens NAMADD with REFI index, and uses label NA
Option 4 is dealt with in Task 26, for now enter: DO PROGREP1
Option 5 is dealt with in Task 27, using a View file. For now omit it.
Option 6 is dealt with in Task 28; for now, enter: DO PROGSTAT
Option 9 returns the user to the main menu
Any other value entered by the user should result in their being asked and allowed to re-input their option.
After processing any option (bar 9) the menu should be redisplayed for further selection(s).
A sample possible solution can be found in the program listing near the end of this Task.

Activity 24.2

Run the program to test all possible options, correct and incorrect, firstly on its own and then from BAS.prg.
For further practice, you could build a further choice into options 1 and 2, either to print out the whole file or to display a given customer's details.

```
****    PROGREPO
****    ACTIVITY 24
****    Reports options
CLEAR
STORE " " TO opt2
DO WHILE .NOT. opt2 = "9"
   CLEAR
   STORE " " TO opt2
   @00,72 SAY "ProgREPO"
   @02,24 SAY "BUDGET ACCOUNT SYSTEM"
   @03,24 SAY "---------------------"
   @05,20 SAY "Select one of the following:"
   @07,20 SAY "1   Name and Address Print"
   @08,20 SAY "2   Transactions Listing"
   @09,20 SAY "3   Address Labels"
   @10,20 SAY "4   Departmental Summary"
   @11,20 SAY "5   Customers' Credit Status Report"
   @12,20 SAY "6   Customer Statements"
   @14,20 SAY "9   Return to Main Menu"
   @16,24 SAY "ENTER OPTION NUMBER HERE: " GET opt2 PICTURE "@Z"
   @18,20 SAY "Check that the printer is online"
   READ
   DO CASE
        CASE opt2 = "1"
             USE namadd INDEX refi
             REPORT FORM narep1 TO PRINT
        CASE opt2 = "2"
             USE trans INDEX trefi
             REPORT FORM tranrep1 TO PRINT
        CASE opt2 = "3"
             USE namadd INDEX refi
             LABEL FORM na SAMPLE TO PRINT
        CASE opt2 = "4"
             DO progrep1
        CASE opt2 = "5"
             @19,10 SAY "OPTION 5 NOT YET AVAILABLE"
             WAIT
             LOOP
        CASE opt2 = "6"
             DO PROGSTAT
        CASE opt = "9"
             EXIT
        OTHERWISE
             @19,10 SAY "INCORRECT OPTION - PLEASE TRY AGAIN"
             WAIT
             LOOP
    ENDCASE
    CLOSE DATABASES
ENDDO
RETURN
****    End of PROGREPO
```

Key words Do 18, 20, 24

Task 25 Programming: using more than one database and updating from another database

Objective

To open and use more than one database at the same time; to update one database with data from another database.

Instructions

Your processing so far has dealt with either NAMADD or TRANS, never both together, but there will be instances when you need to have both files open.
NAMADD.dbf holds a field, BAL, which contains the customer's current balance, but this field has not yet been altered to keep it in line automatically, with the transactions recorded in TRANS.

Activity 25.1

Ignoring for now the question of when this would best be done, for the purposes of this task build an automatic BAL update into the monthend processing in program 21 PROGMTHO.prg (selected as Option 8 by the user).
Enter the program and test it as shown in the program that follows.

```
****     PROGMTHO
****     ACTIVITY 25.1
****     For each  customer on the name and address file:
****     Update their BALance field in NAMADD with the net total of
****     their transaction amounts from TRANS

@15,25 SAY "Updating Customer balances on NAMADD ..."
SELECT 2
USE TRANS
SELECT 1
USE NAMADD
INDEX ON ref TO refi
UPDATE ON ref FROM trans REPLACE bal WITH bal+trans->amount RANDOM
CLOSE DATABASES
RETURN
****     End of ProgMTHO / Program 21 ****
```

Note 1 Select

Format: SELECT <work area/alias>

When you open a database, it is allocated a work area in the computer memory for itself and its associated (.NDX, .SCR, etc) files. This area becomes the 'active work area'. Where your processing involves only one database at a time you need not worry about this.

However, if you intend to use more than one database at the same time, each must be allocated a separate work area, from the ten which are available. These areas can be referenced as 1 to 10 or as A to J.

The SELECT command allows you to specify work areas when opening the databases, and then to swap between them.

In this progam, areas 1 and 2 are reserved for NAMADD and TRANS respectively. Two databases are open, but the active work area is 1 as this is the latest to be selected, and the database currently in use is therefore NAMADD.

If you wish to use fields from another database record in conjunction with the active database record, those fieldnames must be qualified to identify their source.

In the program PROGMTH0 an example of a field qualifier can be found in the UPDATE command, where the AMOUNT field from the second database is written as TRANS–AMOUNT.

When multiple files are opened they can each be given an 'alias'. This alias can then be used to qualify fieldnames. For example, the program could have opened Trans with: USE TRANS ALIAS TR in which case the WITH clause could have read: WITH BAL+TR–>AMOUNT.

If no alias is specified, the filename or the area reference (1,2,3,A,B,C,etc) is used.

Note 2 Update

UPDATE ON <key> FROM <alias> REPLACE <field> WITH <exp> [RANDOM]

This matches the active database with the alias database, record for record, on the key field, and updates the specified field(s). The active database being updated must be indexed or sorted on the key field. The alias must be likewise, unless RANDOM is specified.

Activity 25.2

To test your program, first establish what is on each of the files as follows:
Print out REF and BAL from the name and address file.
Open and then Index TRANS on REF
To obtain the net transactions total for each customer, the TOTAL command can be used. Its format is:
TOTAL ON <keyfield> TO <file> [WHILE/FOR<condition>] [FIELDS<list>]

Note The file being totalled must be indexed or sorted on the keyfield. Numeric fields, either all or only those specified in the FIELDS parameter, from each record are totalled until a change of key is detected. A single record for that last key is then created on the TO file. The whole file is processed in this way, unless a scope or the WHILE/FOR options specify otherwise. At the end, the TO file contains one record for each key.

```
Type TOTAL ON ref TO trans2
     USE TRANS2
     LIST REF, AMOUNT TO PRINT
```

You now have the pre-test values on each database.
One further useful precaution will be to make a copy of the name and address file in its current state. Copy it to NAMADD2.DBF.

Type CLEAR ALL

Run PROGMTH0, then list REF and BAL again, to check that the balances have been correctly updated.

Key words	
	Databases 1, 2, 10, 111
	List 3, 7, 9, 18
	Select
	Total 26
	Copy File 5
	Update on
	Keyfield Intro, 11

Task 26

Programming: joining two databases to create a third

Objective

To learn how to create an additional database from the contents of two existing files.

Instructions

With the JOIN command you can create a new database from the contents of two others. You can specify which fields to include in the new database records, and which records are to be selected. The format is:

JOIN WITH <alias> TO <filename> FOR <condition> [FIELDS <list>]

JOIN matches records from two databases together and for each match where the FOR condition holds creates a record containing the fields specified in the FIELDS parameter.

It reads a record from the active database, and for each record on the alias file which matches the FOR condition, creates a new record on the TO file. It then proceeds to the next record in the active file and repeats the process, and so on until all records have been processed. This could obviously take a long time for large files.

This is illustrated in Activity 26.2, but before that, carry out the following activity.

Activity 26.1

Create a new database, DEPCODES, with records containing just two fields: DEPT (3 characters) and DESCRIPT (20 characters)
This will be a simple reference file of department names.
Insert the following records:

DEPT	DESCRIPT
CF	Children's Fashions
CHI	China & Glass
ELE	Electrical goods
FUR	Furnishings
GF	Gents Fashions
LF	Ladies' Fashions
PER	Perfumery
TOY	Toys & Stationery

Activity 26.2

Open and index TRANS on department to DEPI.ndx
Total on DEPT to DEPTOT
Join DEPTOT and DEPCODES with the commands:

```
SELECT 2
USE DEPTOT
SELECT 1
USE DEPCODES
JOIN WITH B TO newdep FOR dept = B->dept FIELDS dept,descript,B->amount
```

Print out NEWDEP'S contents and its structure.

Activity 26.3 Type CLOSE DATABASES.
Create the report form DEPSUM which uses NEWDEP.dbf to print out the BUDGET ACCOUNT SYSTEM : DEPARTMENTAL SALES SUMMARY, showing department descriptions and sales totals, double-line spaced.

Activity 26.4 Write Program 22: PROGREP1 to print this departmental summary. As the transaction file will be constantly changing, all the commands you carried out in exercise 2 above will have to be part of the program too, preceding the REPORT FORM command. At the beginning of these commands, put SET SAFETY OFF, and at the end of the program, prior to RETURN, put SET SAFETY ON.
Setting safety off stops the program from asking the 'File already exists, overwrite it? Y/N' question.
Test the program on its own, and then via BAS.PRG, option 4 (Reports) option 4 (Dept. Summary).
To see the effect of SAFETY OFF remove this statement and run the program again. Remember to edit back in again afterwards.
A sample possible solution is shown in the following program listing.

```
****    PROGREP1
****    ACTIVITY 26.4
****    Print Departmental summary

CLEAR
SET SAFETY OFF
@20,20 SAY "Processing and Printing Departmental Summary..."
USE trans
INDEX ON dept TO depi
TOTAL ON dept TO deptot
SELECT 2
USE deptot
SELECT 1
USE depcodes
JOIN WITH B TO newdep FOR dept = b->dept FIELDS dept,descript,B->amount
CLOSE DATABASES
USE newdep
REPORT FORM depsum TO PRINT
CLEAR
SET SAFETY ON
RETURN
****    End of PROGREP1 /Program 22  ****
```

Key words	Close databases Create 1, 12, 16, 17, 26 Join Set safety

Task 27 Programming: viewing multiple databases

Objective

To learn how to create a VIEW file and use it to link information from two or more databases.

Instructions

dBASE III provides a very useful VIEW facility which enables you to open multiple databases and their related files with a single instruction. First create a View file in the edit mode, which allows you to select databases, their index and format files, and pick only the fields necessary from each. The view is saved to a file with .VUE appended to its name. Whenever you wish to open those files together in that particular way again, you SET VIEW TO the viewfile.

This is a simplified way of selecting and opening databases, setting the RELATION between them, and using only the FIELDS you require from each.

Create a view of NAMADD and TRANS2 (the file holding transaction totals) in a view file named VIEW1.vue, then create a report form and produce the first of the budget account system's reports, using VIEW1.frm.

Activity 27.1

Creating VIEW1

Type CREATE VIEW VIEW1
SET UP in the menu bar, and a list of your databases is displayed. Use the arrow keys to move the cursor down and then select TRANS2.DBF as the first 'parent' file in the view, and when the indexes are displayed select TREFI.NDX
Arrow left to select NAMADD.DBF as the 'child' file, and its index file REFI.NDX
Use the right-arrow keys to move onto the RELATE menu option, and select TRANS2
Alongside this will appear the NAMADD name and at the bottom of the screen will appear RELATION CHAIN:
Press RETURN, type REF in the space provided, and press RETURN
'Relation chain: Trans2.dbf–>Namadd.dbf' will be displayed at the bottom of screen.
Use arrow keys to move onto and then select the SET FIELDS menu option.
The TRANS2 fields will be displayed already selected as indicated by the small arrows alongside each. We require only REF and AMOUNT, so press RETURN against the other fieldnames to unselect them.
Press the right, then down arrow keys, RETURN to select NAMADD fields. Of these you only require FIRSTNAME, SURNAME, OPENED, CRLIM, and BAL.
Unselect the rest.
Use the arrow keys to move onto and select the EXIT SAVE menu option. This will store the viewfile VIEW1.VUE on disk, and leaves it open for your next activity.

Activity 27.2 Creating report form

Type CREATE REPORT VIEW1
Options:
Set up page title as: BUDGET ACCOUNT SYSTEM

CUSTOMER STATUS REPORT

Set the left margin to 10, double-line spacing, with no page eject before printing.
COLUMNS:
For each column, do the following:
Press **RETURN** to select contents,
press **F10** to list the possible fields,
use arrow/return to select the required field(s)
Press **RETURN**
Select Headings and set them up as indicated below
PGDN to move onto next column.

Col 1 REF — Heading: "Ref'ce"

Col 2 Select FIRSTNAME and then SURNAME from the F10 list, then edit the contents (INS should be on) to read:
LEFT(NAMADD–>FIRSTNAME,1)+" "+NAMADD–>SURNAME

Heading: " Name"

COL 3 OPENED — Heading: "Account Opened"

Col 4 AMOUNT and set its width to 10 — Heading: " Current Balance"

Col 5 CRLIM — Heading: "Credit Limit"

Select the EXIT SAVE options from menu bar to store the form file VIEW1.FRM on disk.

Activity 27.3 Alter PROGREP0 so that CASE opt = "5" reads:

```
CASE opt = "5"
  SET VIEW TO VIEW1
  REPORT FORM VIEW1 TO PRINT
```

Test the program for option 5, by running it on its own and from BAS.prg.

Key words	Create 1, 12, 16, 17, 26 File 1, 2, 11, 12, 16, 17, 19 Menu bar 12, 17 Modify 6, 12, 16, 17, 18, 21 Report 12, 13, 14 Set view View

Task 28

Programming: final exercises

Objective

To print (month end statements) using relative print row addressing
To alter PROGMTHO to clear TRANS of all records.
To learn how to use the macro substitution function

Instructions

The purpose of the last task is to tie up the loose ends of your 'budget account system'. This means writing the program to print out customer statements, and clearing down the transactions file at the month end.

A sample program PROGSTAT follows Activity 28.1, but try your own first: this will give you the opportunity to put into practice all that you have learned. However, there are several extra functions that you might find useful when printing the statements, which were used in the sample program and are described here.

PROW() determines the current row number on the printer.
Type ? PROW()

This function is useful in programs for printing on a row RELATIVE to the last one used. In Program 23, PROGSTAT, it is used in @SAY commands to print out transactions, e.g. @PROW()+3,10 SAY "Transaction Department" prints three lines on from the current position. It is also used to ensure that the closing balance line is printed at row 50, irrespective of how many transaction lines have been printed:

```
  LNCT = 50 – PROW()
  @PROW()+LNCT,20 SAY "Closing Balance"
```

This is an over-simplification, in that some customers may have statements running beyond line 50, but the same function could be used to deal with that check too.

Found() is used with any of the commands which locate a particular record (FIND, SEEK, LOCATE, CONTINUE), to check whether a record was found. It can be used with IF or DO WHILE to repeat the processing for a number of records with the same key. In PROGSTAT the TRANS database is indexed on REF. The first record for the required customer is found using SEEK, then subsequent transactions found with SKIP, e.g:

```
  SEEK "S001"
  IF FOUND()
    DO WHILE ref = "S001"
    processing ...
    ... processing
    SKIP
    ENDDO
  ENDIF
```

Eject is a dBASE command which causes a page-throw on the printer, and resets the value of PROW() to zero.

& This function is used to substitute the contents of the given variable for its name. This is useful when you want to vary the value on different occasions, but still use the same program. An example is where you want to specify the name of a file to be opened:

```
  ACCEPT 'Please enter name of file to be processed: 'to FNAME
USE &FNAME
```

In PROGSTAT it is used in the SEEK statement after the user has specified a customer reference:

```
  GET whichone
  SEEK "&WHICHONE"
```

Activity 28.1 Write Program 23, PROGSTAT, to print out the statement of account for a customer, whose reference is to be specified by the user at runtime. A possible layout is shown at the end of this activity. If you wish to use a layout of your own, make sure you have a written plan of it before you start programming.

In the sample program, a report form was used to print the top half of the statement dealing with the headings, name, address, and reference, as shown, but this is not necessary. If you do the same, set page ejects off and set to plain page.

Test PROGSTAT When satisfied that it works, test via BAS.PRG.

A sample possible solution is shown below.

```
****    progstat.PRG
****    ACTIVITY 28.1
****    Prints or displays Month-end Statements
CLEAR ALL
SET TALK OFF
SET DATE BRITISH
SET SAFETY OFF
CLEAR
STORE "     " TO whichone
@10,15 SAY " Month End Statement "
@12,15 SAY " Enter Customer Reference : " GET whichone PICTURE "@! A999"
READ
SELECT 1
USE NAMADD
INDEX ON REF TO REFI
LOCATE FOR ref = whichone
REPORT FORM STAT1 next 1 TO PRINT
mbal = NAMADD->BAL
SET DEVICE TO PRINT
@PROW()+3,10 SAY "Transaction Department"
@PROW(),42 SAY "Date           Amount"
SELECT 2
USE TRANS
INDEX ON REF TO TREFI
SEEK "&whichone"
IF FOUND()
  DO WHILE trans->ref = "&whichone"
    @PROW()+1,10 SAY trans->rec
    @PROW(),20 SAY trans->dept
    @PROW(),42 SAY trans->tdate
    @PROW(),55 SAY trans->amount
    mbal = mbal+trans->amount
    SKIP
  ENDDO
ENDIF
lnct = 50-prow()
@PROW()+lnct,20 SAY "           Closing Balance "+STR(mbal,8,2)
eject
SET DEVICE TO SCREEN
SET SAFETY ON
CLEAR ALL
RETURN
```

Activity 28.2 Once the update of current balance has been carried out, clear down the transactions file at monthend.
Alter PROGMTH0 to delete all records from TRANS . It would be wise to issue the PACK command later.

Activity 28.3 For further practice, modify your program so that it prints out the statements for all customers.

Key words

- &
- Function 7, 9, 15, 16
- Pack 5
- Prow

Possible layout:

BUDGET ACCOUNT

STATEMENT OF ACCOUNT

xxxxxxx-Name-xxxxxxxxxxx xxxxxxx-Address-xxxx

xxxxxxxxxxxxxxxxxxx

A/C Ref: A999 xxxxxxxxxxxxxxxxxxx

xxxxxxxxxxxxxxxxxxx

Date: dd/mm/yy

Transaction	Dept	Date	Amount
xxx	xxx	dd/mm/yy	9999.99
xxx	xxx	dd/mm/yy	9999.99
xxx	xxx	dd/mm/yy	9999.99
xxx	xxx	dd/mm/yy	9999.99
xxx	xxx	dd/mm/yy	9999.99
xxx	xxx	dd/mm/yy	9999.99
xxx	xxx	dd/mm/yy	9999.99
xxx	xxx	dd/mm/yy	9999.99

[etc etc one line for each transaction]

Closing Balance : 9999.99

Conclusion

This Training Guide has concentrated on the dBASE commands and functions. Having mastered the language, you will soon find that the program coding is more of a clerical job than anything else: the most important part is in the planning and documenting of the system.

There are numerous books giving further advice on the design of databases and programs. In particular, for further practice in using dBASE III +, the Ashton-tate manual is a useful reference.

Appendix

Program Listings

Programs developed in the training guide

Sequence	Name	Description	Task No
Program 1	ProgNA1	Amend customer record	18
Program 2	ProgNA2	Insert new customer record	18
Program 3	ProgNA3	Delete customer record	18
Program 4	ProgTR1	Input a Purchase record	19
Program 5	ProgTR2	Input a Payment record	19
Program 6	ProgTR3	Input a Returns record	19
Program 7	ProgTR0	Select & process Purchase or Payment	20
Program 8	ProgNA0	Select & process Amend or Insert record	20
Program 9	ProgTR0	Select Purchase Payment or Return	21
Program 10	ProgNA0	Select Amend Insert or delete record	21
Program 11	ProgTR0	Repeat Selection (Pur Pay Ret)	22
Program 12	ProgNA0	Repeat Selection (Amend Insert Delete)	22
Program 13	Bas	Main system menu for all options+extras	23
Program 14	ProgTR0	Altered for called by/do WITH	23
Program 15	ProgTR1	Altered for called by/do WITH	23
Program 16	ProgNA0	Altered for called by/do WITH	23
Program 17	ProgNA1	Cleared of redundant commands	23
Program 18	ProgNA2		23
Program 19	ProgNA3		23
Program 20	ProgREP0	Reports Selection Menu	24
Program 21	ProgMTH0	Monthend processing	25, 28
Program 22	ProgREP1	Print Departmental Summary	26
Program 23	ProgSTAT	Print monthend Statements	28